POWER PITCHES

How to Produce Winning Presentations Using Charts, Slides, Video & Multimedia

POWER PITCHES

How to Produce Winning Presentations Using Charts, Slides, Video & Multimedia

ALAN L. BROWN

IRWIN
Professional Publishing
Chicago • London • Singapore

McGraw-Hill
    A Division of the McGraw-Hill Companies

POWER PITCHES: HOW TO PRODUCE WINNING PRESENTATIONS
USING CHARTS, SLIDES, VIDEO AND MULTIMEDIA

This publication is designed to provide accurate and authoritative information
in regard to the subject matter covered. It is sold with the understanding that
neither the author or the publisher is engaged in rendering legal, accounting,
or other professional service. If legal advice or other expert assistance is
required, the services of a competent professional person should be sought.

*From a Declaration of Principles jointly adopted by a Committee of the
American Bar Association and a Committee of Publishers.*

1 2 3 4 5 6 7 8 9 0 DOC DOC 3 2 1 0 9 8 7 6

Library of Congress Cataloging-in-Publication Data

Brown, Alan L.
    Power pitches : how to produce winning presentations using charts,
slides, video, and multimedia / Alan L. Brown
        p.   cm.
    Includes index.
    ISBN: 0-7863-0972-5
    1. Sales presentations—Graphic methods.   2. Multimedia systems
in business presentations.   I. Title
HF5438.8.P74 B76   1997
658.85—dc21   96-48063

For Lori,
who makes every day a
wondrous, loving adventure.

PREFACE

Yes. You Can Deliver a Business Presentation People Won't Soon Forget. This book was written especially for business people who are required to make formal or informal presentations to sell ideas, concepts, products, or services. Reading it will dramatically improve your ability to organize, produce, and deliver those presentations. Sharpening those skills is especially important as computer-driven presentations become more and more common to the workplace. This book's goals, while not modest, are readily attainable. Fundamentally, I want to teach you the principles of good business presentations (The Ten Rules of Power Pitching) and show you how to use the "language of visual communications" to make your presentations more powerful. Don't be misled; this is not a "how to" book. I am not going to teach you how to make a slide. *But I am going to teach how to make powerful presentations.*

I will cover the visual support spectrum: flip charts, overhead transparencies, 35mm slides, videotape and computer generated presentations (multimedia)—all very powerful tools when used artfully. I'll also discuss proper presentation organization, techniques for evaluating and directing creative output, and how to manage creative resources.

As I'll remind you from time to time, this is a book you'll want to read now, and then keep on your bookshelf to refer to later when you're preparing important presentations. I don't believe you can find a more comprehensive, easier to use source on this subject. Stick with it, and your presentations will keep getting better and better. Your confidence will soar—you'll gain more sales opportunities, close more deals, motivate more forcefully, and educate more effectively. Really.

ACKNOWLEDGMENTS

I am deeply indebted to Wayne McGuirt and Jeffrey Krames for providing me with the opportunity—and world-class support—to write this book.

I want to give special recognition to two people who contributed so richly to the final product: Patrick Muller, my developmental editor, whose insight, patience, prodding, and sense of humor kept me on course; and Elizabeth Sinkler, who so generously supported me with her time, expert criticism, and the resources of her firm (the majority of the graphics in this book were created by her company, Sinkler or Sinkler, Inc.—"SOS" as it's so aptly referred to in the business community).

I would like to thank Ron Carlson, Steve Gilberg, Val Mrak, and Andrea Zorn who, when called upon, helped me solve problems or answer questions that related to specific segments of this book. I also wish to thank my family and friends for their unqualified support, encouragement and tolerance. Special thanks to: Louis, The Count, Susie Q, Tall Nick, Cute Nick, Sammy, Marty, Ross, and Max.

Finally, I want to pay tribute to my mother who watched over me from Elysian Fields and was there for me whenever I needed to borrow some of her strength or wisdom. Thanks Mom, I hope you like the book.

Alan L. Brown

CONTENTS

Chapter 3

Speaking the Visual Language   59

Chapter 4

Power Pitching   87

Chapter 5

Primary Presentation Media   105

Chapter 6

Video: The Most Powerful Presentation Medium of All   131

Chapter 7

Working with Creative Resources   177

PROLOGUE

THE POWER OF VISUAL COMMUNICATIONS

Lewis McClure, one of my professors at the University of Illinois Business School turned me on to the advertising business. A prepossessing former New York City ad guy with a thick mane of white hair and a dry martini sense of humor, he would often hold court across the street from Gregory Hall before our 8:00 A.M. class. Here, over bad coffee and doughnuts, he would regale us with wonderful stories about the advertising business and the world of Madison Avenue—an exciting, glamorous, exhilarating world as he portrayed it. A world I desperately wanted to join.

Ultimately, when it came to my getting into the advertising business, Professor McClure had two pieces of advice for me. "First," he said, "when you graduate, get a sales job; you can't be a great marketer if you don't understand the real 'guts' of selling—the frustrations, the rejections, the high highs, and low lows. Besides, selling is a great way for people just out of school to learn to think on their feet. Hell, what do you know about the real business world anyway?" Then he cautioned, "*And* stay away from those agency training programs; usually they try to trick you into staying in the media department, or worse, turn you into a PR guy." Professor McClure had a brooding dislike for media people and PR guys. We never knew why, but we speculated it may have had something to do with an ex-wife. You know those ad guys.

My first job out of college was selling ad space for the *Chicago Tribune*. It was a great first job—lots of prestige, decent money ($105 a week, a tidy wage for 1966), and a collegial, high-spirited, competitive atmosphere.

I had been calling on this furniture dealer—who ran *all* his ads in the hated *Sun Times* Sunday magazine section—for almost a year. I couldn't even sell him a want ad. Although he would agree to see me from time to time, I just couldn't get close to him. He didn't eat lunch, play golf, or drink (I bet you think I'm making this up). Small talk bored him; whenever I tried it, he would quickly become distracted and boot me. If I eschewed the schmoozing and went directly to business, my presentation would always come off forced, hurried, lacking sincerity. He would boot me before I could even get close to asking for an order. This guy was driving me nuts. I had to convince him that he was advertising in the wrong paper.

Perhaps I subconsciously recalled the aphorism about the worth of a picture in words because, one Sunday, I was inspired to cut out a bunch of ads from the *Sun Times* and paste them on a board to create a sort of montage of "schlocky" advertisers. Next, I built a montage of ads strategically selected from the *Tribune*'s magazine section and pasted the collection next to the *Sun Times* montage. Then I pasted a black, 6-inch equilateral triangle in the middle of the *Sun Times* montage and a black, 6-by-8-inch rectangle in the middle of the *Tribune* montage. Finally, after labeling each montage, I cut out the furniture dealer's 6-by-8-inch rectangular ad and centered it over and between the two montages followed by a big hand-lettered "where do you fit in?" Schematically, it looked something like this:

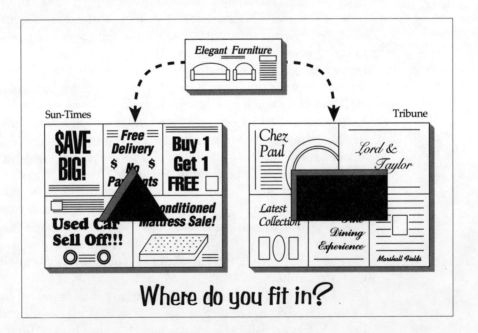

On Monday I called my "friendly antagonist," the furniture dealer, to see if he could spare two minutes to see me. He told me to stop by after lunch. That afternoon I marched into his store with my board. I ceremoniously unwrapped it, handed it to him, and asked him to seriously consider the question. Then I thanked him and left. Two days later I got a call from him asking me to stop by; seems he's been considering an ad schedule in the *Tribune*. That was my first exposure to the power of visual communications.

The Power of Visual Communications Redux

About six months after the furniture-dealer caper, I was in hot pursuit of my dream job—an ad agency account executive slot at Earle Ludgin & Company, working on the Sealy Posturepedic account. Sealy was a national advertiser, and that meant network TV! Ludgin was one of the hottest shops in town, boasting creative teams recruited from New York where agencies like Doyle, Dane & Bernbach and Young & Rubicam were doing ground breaking creative work and turning the agency business on its head. It seemed to me like everyone in Chicago wanted this job. The hiring process was tortuous, but after three intense interviews I made the short list. One final round of interviews to go. Bob Pingrey, the account supervisor, was giving each finalist one last opportunity to convince the agency that he had the most smarts, tenacity, discipline, creativity, or whatever it was Ludgin was looking for to win the job. My challenge was to differentiate myself from the others whom, I presumed, had formidable skills and talent. I struggled with that problem for a couple of days: Had I done anything so far in my brief career—beyond winning a few sales contests—that would impress Bob and convince him that I was the *only* man for the job?

I found the answer in the trunk of my car. There, under a layer of soiled team uniforms, worn long ago, and my collection of useless things, just slightly crumpled, was the board I had reclaimed from "my good buddy," the furniture dealer. Would Bob be impressed, or would he consider it hokey? Figuring it couldn't hurt, I brought the board to the final interview. I told him my story and showed him the *slightly* crumpled board.

Bob was impressed. He made me an ad guy.

The Power of Visual Communications (Continued)

By 1975 I had shifted to the client side of the business. I was director of marketing for Motorola's Consumer Product Division, after having been hired as its director of advertising in 1972. "Presentations" to customers, distributors, subordinates, superiors, outside resources, and interest groups of all kinds were part of my life. And frankly, I got to be pretty good at it. I took to heart the lessons I learned early about the power of visual communications and never missed the opportunity to take advantage of it.

That same year Motorola decided to sell the Consumer Products Division to Matsushita, an event that gave me the opportunity to team up with Don Wallace, an incredibly talented and perceptive creative director and filmmaker I had worked with at Clinton E. Frank Advertising, and Gene Rosner, a brilliant, exceptionally skilled Bohemian graphic designer I had met in the army. (Gene was the worst soldier I ever knew.) We proposed forming a company that would provide traditional audiovisual services (TV commercials, industrial films, and sales meeting support) as well as graphic design (brochures, annual reports, and collateral of all kinds). In addition, we would pursue nonbroadcast videotape production—we agreed there was a tremendous opportunity to exploit the potential of this medium (½-inch video was still a nascent industry). I would handle operations and sales; Don and Gene would run creative and production of their respective areas of expertise. But before I would agree to our alliance, I made them promise to include me in the creative process. I was convinced my marketing training and experience, in concert with my conceptual skills, would give our company a significant competitive edge.

It was a heady experience. Our firm (Brown & Rosner as it became in 1978) grew to become one of the most respected graphic design and audiovisual resources in town. Don and Gene had taught me well.

And now, with videotape players just about as common to the workplace as fax machines, and the rapid emergence of electronic imaging and computerized presentations, I felt it was time to bring some order and discipline to the art of business presentation organization and visualization.

This book will *empower* you to make presentations that will enthrall your audiences and distinguish you from your competition. And that's not an idle promise.

POWER PITCHES

How to Produce Winning Presentations Using Charts, Slides, Video & Multimedia

CHAPTER 1

Introduction to Business Presentations

1.1 BEAR WITH ME—IT'S NOT AS DRY OR TEDIOUS AS IT SOUNDS

In 1989 my oldest daughter was awarded a Bachelor's Degree in Advertising from a well-respected Big Ten university. As you might expect, I was both flattered and proud that she had chosen to follow her dad's career path. Although we talked regularly about her studies during her four years at school, it wasn't until the *exact* day of her graduation that I realized she had not taken a basic marketing course. It wasn't a degree requirement. I went hyper-space. I recall carrying on for weeks, griping to my friends and associates that offering an advertising degree without a marketing 101 requirement would be like training doctors to be heart specialists without giving them some rudimentary knowledge of the circulatory system. Finally, I wrote a very pleasant, well-intentioned letter (OK, maybe it was just a hair acerbic) to the dean of the college demanding an explanation. My letter was never answered and my daughter became a school-teacher. She hated advertising.

Accordingly, before we can get into the specifics and nuances of business presentations, we need talk about the "circulatory system"— we need to examine and agree upon some basic terms and concepts.

1

We'll begin by reviewing what we all should have learned in Marketing 101 (unless of course you went to the same school as my daughter)—the four categories of business presentations.

1.2 THE FOUR PRESENTATION TYPES

If you think about it, you generally have one of four objectives in mind when you make a presentation: to educate, instruct, provoke, or motivate. Consequently, there are four categories of business presentations:

1. Educational   Provide information for its own sake.
2. Instructional   Teach methods or procedures.
3. Provocational   Offer information or concepts to encourage constructive criticism and the exchange of ideas.
4. Motivational   Cause specific action(s) to be taken or behavior to be modified.

Let's take a look a closer look at each of these categories.

Educational Presentations

Presentations that are educational or informational in nature are principally driven by the need to introduce audiences to certain facts or conditions relative to the policies, products, or services of the business organization. Response or action on the part of the audience may or may not be required. Successful educational presentations require clarity of thought and ideas and must be able to maintain listener interest. Examples of educational presentations include policy changes or introductions (e.g., a new retirement program or profit-sharing plan); performance status or results (e.g., sales manager or shareholder meetings); and matters of price or payment terms relative to products or services.

Instructional Presentations

Instructional presentations are common in the workplace. They range from the simple ("how to fill out a form") to the abstruse ("how to build your own computer"). To be effective, instructional presentations must be intelligible and precise with respect to the information being imparted. Obviously, visuals can contribute mightily to their success.

Provocational Presentations

Provocational presentations are intended to stimulate an audience's thinking for the purpose of either developing, executing, or revising a specific action or set of actions. Examples include reviews of developmental business plans to senior managers and staff; financial reports to corporate boards; and creative output presentations to clients by advertising or promotional agencies. Note that in the examples I just cited, evoking ideas, perceptions, emotions, or valuations and gaining feedback—the ultimate goal of a provocational presentation—are the desired results of the presenter.

Motivational Presentations

Arguably, motivation is inherent in all presentations to one degree or another. Sales presentations, by definition, are first-degree motivational presentations. Ultimately, they have only one goal—*motivating* the prospect or customer to award you the "business." Motivational presentations are the raison d'etre of this book. In fact, I'd bet "wanting to win more business" is why you bought this book in the first place. If you had some other reason, please write me and let me know what it was.

1.3 PRESENTATION AUDIENCES: WHO ARE THESE GUYS?

Understanding the audience is essential to creating powerful business presentations. It's a subject we'll discuss at length. But first, let's deal with the basics. We're going to divide business presentation audiences into two discrete groups, internal and external; then we'll further divide external audiences into sales and nonsales types as follows:

◆ Internal Audiences

Limited to employees or distribution factors (distributors, reps, dealers) of a business organization.

◆ External Audiences/Nonsales

All outside resources (other than distribution factors, e.g., attorneys, advertising agents, PR firms) plus financial analysts, shareholders/investors, and media.

◆ External Audiences/Sales

Current customers and prospects.

Let's dig deeper—power presentations demand knowing everything you can about your audience. To help accomplish that goal, let's further break down External Audiences/Sales into two subclassifications: decision makers and influencers:

Decision Makers

These are the people who have the *authority* to make the purchase decision.

Influencers

These people, as the classification title implies, wield great *influence* with respect to the ultimate purchase decision but lack the authority to make that decision unilaterally. Never *ever* underestimate or trivialize the importance of influencers in the decision-making process. If your presentation favorably impresses an influencer, it could make the difference between winning the business or whining about what might have been.

Knowing the role each person plays in the decision-making process gives you important presentation direction—you especially want to "connect" with the decision maker without disaffecting yourself from others who may be involved in the process. If you are presenting to a decision-making committee, try to understand the dynamics (read "politics") of the group. Don't forget to find out if your "contact" at that client or prospect (in the case of external sales presentations) is in a position to provide you with any valuable insight.

Early in my career I pitched a project to a small, mixed group of four or five managers and a VP. I had neglected to do my homework and knew very little about the audience. Instinctively, I directed my remarks and witty asides to the big cheese. Later I found out he was invited as a courtesy and had absolutely nothing to do with making the final decision. Whoo, I really vexed those managers. Not only didn't we get the job, our firm was never invited to bid on another project. Moral: When in doubt play the room.

Analyzing the complexion of your audience and the role each person plays in the decision-making process is where the presentation creative process begins. We'll discuss this process in greater detail in Chapter 2.

1.4 THE LANGUAGE OF VISUAL COMMUNICATIONS

Going back to my first experience with the power of visual communications, I eventually came to realize that visualization is actually a language—a language that allows you to communicate with precision and impact. It's not unlike the English language where adjectives, adverbs, and descriptive clauses add to our understanding of the message we're receiving. Take a moment to develop a visual picture in your mind after reading each of the following phrases:

1. It's raining.
2. It's raining hard.
3. Rain gushed from the sky as thunder roared and lightning crashed around us.
4. It's raining like a banana.

Clearly, the addition of the *right* words or phrases allows our imaginations to create more precise (powerful?) mental pictures. The *wrong* words or phrases can create confusion.

The language of visual communications has four principal components—these components can stand alone or work in concert with one another:

- ◆ TEXT
  Words or copy that help inform, embellish, clarify, support, or distinguish.
- ◆ RECOGNIZABLE SYMBOLS
  Visual impressions of *known* signs or representations that create impact, interest or add memorability.
- ◆ CHARTS AND GRAPHS
  An organized presentation of information in various formats (tables, maps, lines, bars, curves) representing historic or projected data, functions, or relationships.
- ◆ IMAGERY
  Photographs or graphic representations (illustrations) that create settings and moods or trigger emotions.

Figure 1–1 provides examples of visual language components in the context of presentations.

Connotation is both the nature and strength of visual communications. Be aware that this sword cuts two ways—you can create powerful negative impressions as well. I'll show you how to forcefully "speak" the language of visual communications in Chapter 3.

FIGURE 1–1

Examples of Language of Visual Communications

Text

it's **BIG!**	**BENEFITS:** ° Low Maintenance ° Longer Life ° Environmentally Safe	"...we saved <u>over</u> <u>600</u> <u>hours</u> <u>per</u> <u>month</u> with the Control-A-Matic!"	**THE BEGINNING...**

Symbols

? $ ✌ H₂O ⊘ 🏛 ☆ ◔

H_2O

Charts and Graphs

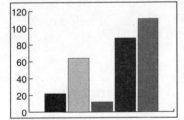 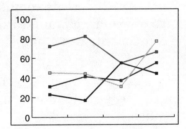 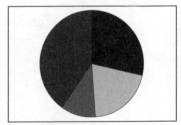

Imagery

Source: S.O.S., Chicago. Used with permission.

1.5 PRESENTATION CHARACTER: THE ELEMENTS OF STYLE, SUBSTANCE AND TONE

If the visual language is the heart of a presentation, then style, substance, and tone are its *soul*—the defining character of a presentation.

Style

Style is about structure. Effectively, there are only three presentation styles: tightly structured, loosely structured, or unstructured. I'm not a big fan of unstructured presentations. I endorse loosely structured presentations—especially to small groups or customers/prospects with whom you have developed a relationship (they know you and what you're about). Tightly structured presentations work best with large groups, especially in cases where many of the faces in the crowd are unfamiliar. Sometimes tightly structured presentations are mandated by the group to whom your presenting. That usually means a competitive situation—you better know what you're doing (keep reading and you will).

♦ *Tightly structured presentations* should be considered formal presentations in the sense the presenter leads the audience to the conclusion. There are no deviations from the "script," and no unsolicited interruptions or questions are encouraged (or desired) until the presentation has been concluded.

♦ *Loosely structured presentations* will generally retain some degree of formality. Although the presenter follows a "script," (more commonly a script outline), comments or questions are encouraged (requested) at strategic points during the presentation.

♦ *Unstructured presentations* are always informal; there is no "script" to follow. Typically, the presenter makes introductory remarks and then allows the audience to lead the presentation. This style can be risky for presenters who are not good extemporaneous speakers, or for anyone who is not well prepared.

Substance

Substance is about content. Please excuse me for stating the obvious, but regardless of the type of presentation you're making, or the audience to whom you're speaking, your presentation needs to be (check four):

___ Timely

___ Factual

___ Interesting

___ Meaningful

If it's not, you've got problems.

Tone

Tone is about personality—the character of the presentation. Unlike presentation styles, presentation tones run the gamut: serious, off-the-cuff, sophisticated, warm, friendly, low key, threatening, confident, cocky, aloof, technical, and so on. You know what tone works best for you; just be sure your audience is receptive—some people like cockiness, some interpret it as arrogance. Nobody likes arrogance. You can also blend tones but be careful—too many tonal shifts will confuse or distract your audience.

I'll be referring to substance, style, and tone throughout this book.

1.6 THE PRESENTATION SUPPORT ARMAMENTARIUM

I maintain that virtually every presentation can and should be enhanced by visual support.

Sometimes business presentations need to be full-blown "dog and pony shows" with a cast of thousands, laser lights, holograms, pyrotechnics, and ear-splitting surround-a-sound. And sometimes, very dramatic presentations are made in a customer's cubicle over a cup of coffee with a number 2 pencil and a big yellow scratch pad. I have sat in the audience of more than a few big-budget sales presentations, watching eyes glaze over and heads bob fighting off the tedium of redundant, rambling speakers plodding through uninspired, unintelligible slides. On the other hand, one of the most successful real estate executives I know pitches (and frequently lands) million-dollar deals using a couple of boards and an easel.

Between these extremes are the tens of thousands of presentations made every day by business people—maybe just like you—trying to sell an idea or win a piece of business. Their presentations are occasionally enhanced by electronic images, videos, slides, overhead transparencies, audio tapes, elaborate sales kits, flip charts, product samples, props, and print materials of all kinds including slick brochures, not-so-slick brochures, catalogs, ad reprints, article reprints, monographs, sell sheets, and price sheets. Sixteen millimeter film and (thankfully) filmstrips are in audiovisual heaven along with 2-inch videotape and wire recorders.

Let's consider the panoply of business presentation support materials and systems at our disposal (Table 1–1). Surveying this landscape will open your mind to all the options available to help support your presentation. And while you may not have direct control over all of these options, certainly the basic presentation tools— boards, overheads, slides, and electronic (PC) images—are within your purview. These media are the primary thrust of this book.

T A B L E 1-1

Business and Sales Presentation Support Grid

Sales Support Tool	General Description	Primary Use	Strengths	Weaknesses
Videotape (small formats: ½" VHS, ¾")	Sight, sound, motion. Can integrate original and existing tape footage, film, stills, computer graphics. Requires ½" VHS video deck and color TV receiver.	Can support initial overview presentation of company/ product/service to small or large group to create interest, establish credibility; also very effective for specific programs, products, or services.	Tremendous flexibility and range—from plant tours to testimonials. Very portable. Can be played in ambient light. Easy to stop, skip, or repeat. Editing allows cost-effective modifications or personalization.	Can be costly to produce. Salespeople may resist using or misuse. Risk of "turning off" customer if video is not well produced (qualitatively), inaccurate, or not believable. Can become dated.
Slides (35mm)	Photos, words or graphics projected to larger-than-life scale. Requires 35mm projector, screen (ideally), and venue that allows optimal setup.	Most frequently used in presentations to larger audiences to introduce company/products/ services.	Can be very high impact when using thoughtful, sophisticated graphics and beautiful photography. Presenter has lots of flexibility with respect to amount of time spent on each slide or subject.	Poorly produced slides can be hard to read and distracting. Requires preparation and rehearsal by presenter(s). Equipment can be problematic—poorly mounted slides can lose focus. Because room must be darkened, intimacy is lost with audience.
Overheads (acetates)	Projection of basic copy, charts, graphs usually generated by computer software program. Requires overhead projector.	Principally used in small group meetings to discuss plans, strategies, details, as well as in traditional sales presentations.	Cost effective. Easy to use. Very flexible (changes can be made in minutes). Helps keep meetings on subject.	Not well suited for motivational-type presentations or very large groups.
Audio Tapes (cassettes)	Direct audio playback. Requires audio cassette player with appropriate sound amplification.	Usually features senior company executives or satisfied customers/ testimonials to augment a presentation. Also used as a leave-behind.	Can be very influential, especially if recorded speaker(s) is well-known and/or highly regarded. Portable; easy to implement.	If not carefully produced, can be tedious; if not believable, can negatively impact a presentation. If used as leave-behind most likely will not be played.
Sales Kits/Flip Charts	Provides flow to presentation: background, introduction, body, conclusions. Ranges from simple to outrageously elaborate.	Desktop format for one-on-one or small group presentations. Boards on an easel can accommodate larger audiences.	Flexible. Encourages dialogue and questions. Keeps presentation on-track.	Some buyers (and salespeople) resist "canned" presentations. Can get dog-eared after extended use. Elaborate kits can be very costly. Salespeople need to be instructed in use.
Props	Modified samples of product (e.g., cut-aways), product components, competitive products, or any relevant tangible object to illustrate point or conclusion.	Highlight feature or benefit claims. Competitive comparisons.	Can be very powerful and involving. Supports assertions.	Can be cumbersome to use or transport. Cynical customers may suspect doctoring or factual misrepresentation.
Product Samples	Actual product (may be specially packed or labeled).	For customer/prospect to examine, test or pass on to end user for feedback.	Snows confidence in product; allows customers to make subjective judgments.	Can be costly or wasteful if samples are misused or misappropriated.

TABLE 1–1

(concluded)

Sales Support Tool	General Description	Primary Use	Strengths	Weaknesses
Comprehensive Brochures	Provides broad information. May be highly detailed. (Ranges from modest to elaborate.)	Principally a leave-behind piece. Difficult to use as a presentation tool (client/prospect easily becomes distracted by reading or thumbing through pages).	Thoughtfully created brochure can create positive impressions. Opportunity to expose audiences to full scope of program or introduce full range of products/services.	Can be costly. Easily outdated. Often mistakenly used as an unsolicited direct-mail piece.
Sell Sheets/"Mini" Brochures (generally more narrowly directed to a specific program, product, product line, or category of service)	Usually newsworthy, targeted to specific audience. Often short-term in nature dealing with a limited time opportunity or offer.	Excellent for one-on-one sales calls. Used either during presentation or as a leave-behind (can be mailed to existing customers if appropriate).	Keeps presenters (especially salespeople) focused. Useful (information driven). Often provides "reason" for presentation. Excellent leave-behind.	Negatives are invariably a function of poor production (poor printing, unflattering photography, rambling copy, grammatical errors, etc.).
Spec Sheet/Price Sheet (product)	Informational in nature; ingredients, sizes, colors, model numbers, technical data, etc. May include features/benefits.	One-on-one, small group, or for mailing to current customers.	Comprehensive purchase/order-ing information.	Limited shelf life.
Catalogs (product)	Usually includes all products offered by company; prices with limited feature/benefit copy; ordering/shipping information.	Leave-behind or mailing item. (Can be referenced in presentation and used as prop.)	Illustrates depth of company. A thoughtfully produced catalog (informative, easy-to-use, current) can positively impact sales.	Can be extremely costly; requires updating. Poorly produced catalog (i.e., difficult to use) can cost sales.
Advertising Reprints (print ads)	Reproduction of current or planned advertising.	Evidences support of products/services. Excellent mailer.	Demonstrates marketing commitment of company. Good ads can positively influence customer/prospect.	Promise to run ads unfilled. Style or content of ads may turn off customer/prospect.
Secondary Source Reprints (articles, monographs, research reports, etc.)	Reproduction of published materials.	Substantiates claims. Informs audiences of issues that support presenter's point of view.	Third-party endorsement (no vested interest). Can be especially powerful if material reflects opinion of respected person, organization, or publication.	Source may be questionable or not believable.
Electronic Imaging (PC)	Hybrid of slides and videotape played on a PC or laptop or projected on a screen using an LCD projection system; more advanced systems can play full-motion video.	Desirable for major presentations or high-frequency presentations for one-on-one or large group audiences.	State-of-the-art—very dramatic. Extremely flexible (can be used with virtually any sized audience). Easily/effectively customized.	Presenters get too involved in graphics at expense of substance. Laptop presentations limited to audiences of two or three people. Hardware, software, and production can be costly and time-consuming.

2 CHAPTER

Power Pitching

The Basics

You have had one or many contacts with your prospect or customer. You have gleaned as much information as possible. You have done your best to process that information and understand the prospect's or customer's needs. Finally, you've been invited to make a sales presentation to win the business. It could be the biggest sale you ever made. You could be rich. You could be famous. But will your presentation be powerful enough to carry the day?

2.1 THE TEN RULES OF POWER PITCHING: AN EPIPHANY

I thought about calling this section something like "a common sense approach to business and sales presentation development." But that title not only lacked panache, it failed to communicate the critical *importance* of this information. *Rules* is a more compelling term. I want to compel you to learn the techniques and to follow the processes I'm about to unfold.

As I mentioned earlier, creating business and sales presentations is something I've been doing most of my professional life—*intuitively*. I became enlightened, however, when I began writing about the creation of powerful business presentations and actually thought about all that I have learned from so many of the masters of this craft and factored in my own years of experience. I'm confident you'll be similarly enlightened. I urge you to take the time to learn and adopt these rules. If you do, you will never make a feckless business presentation again.

The Ten Rules of Power Pitching

Although the Ten Rules of Power Pitching apply to *all* business presentations, I am going to present and expound upon these rules in the context of sales presentations. I'm using this approach because virtually every business presentation *is a sales presentation,* and I want you to think about your presentation from the perspective of "selling something." Think about it. Every time you make a presentation, at a minimum, you're selling yourself. So with that in mind, let's consider the ten business-presentation commandments.

1. Treat every presentation you make as if it's the only shot you're going to get at the "business."
2. Qualify your audience.
3. Determine your presentation objective.
4. Develop your strategic presentation outline.
5. Elaborate content.
6. Create a presentation storyboard.
7. Use visuals to simplify and amplify key points.
8. Plan the media selection, delivery, and staging of your presentation.
9. Produce your presentation visuals in a manner consistent with your presentation objective and strategy.
10. Rehearse. Rehearse.

2.2 RULE ONE: TREAT EVERY SALES PRESENTATION YOU MAKE AS IF IT'S THE ONLY SHOT YOU'RE GOING TO GET AT THE "BUSINESS"

This rule is about discipline. We've all heard the one about the salesman who contemptuously ignored the graceless, grungy, goofy-looking customer only to find out later that the graceless, grungy, goofy-looking geezer was a gazillionaire ready to buy out the store. The moral of that story is obvious (I hope) and can be parabled to every sales milieu.

Rule One is critical to creating *powerful* business presentations. Consider it a point of view—an attitude you need to assume in order to *discipline* yourself to take the time and steps necessary to organize, conceptualize, produce, and deliver a presentation that will really make a positive impression on your audience. The rewards will more than compensate your efforts. Without this discipline it's easy to adopt the "I'll worry about it later" approach (also known as Rule Eleven). For most people, Rule Eleven *is* Rule One. Lucky you.

2.3 RULE TWO: QUALIFY YOUR AUDIENCE

The audience, as I pointed out earlier, drives the presentation's style, substance and tone and provides the platform for devising your presentation objectives and strategies. Here are the variables that most directly influence the content of your presentation and require your attention:

1. **Need** How will the product or service you're selling help the prospect or customer meet its needs (more effectively or efficiently than your competition)?

2. **Knowledge** How well informed is the audience about you and your company's history, resources, capabilities, experience, strengths, etc.?

3. **Expertise** Engineering, manufacturing, finance, marketing—what discipline best defines your audience, or is it a mix of disciplines?

Answering these questions is where you begin the presentation "creative process."

Needs and Desires

Selling is all about satisfying needs. Of all the variables, identifying and comprehending needs is the most critical because it most directly influences your presentation objective. *Good* decision makers are easy to communicate with if you can effectively demonstrate your *understanding* of their needs and desires. With respect to sales presentations, needs and desires are distinguished from each other in this manner: *Needs* are purchase criteria that *must* be met; *desires* are the *optimal fulfillment* of those needs. For example, if your automobile breaks down you *need* a mechanic to fix it. At the same time, you *desire* a mechanic who is knowledgeable about your make of automobile, is available to repair it immediately, has the necessary equipment and parts, is honest and reliable, does excellent work, and charges a fair price. From that perspective, and going back to the point I made earlier about what audiences want to know about you, it's easy to conclude what decision makers want to hear:

- You have a solid grasp of their business/operations.
- The product or service you're selling meets or exceeds their specifications/expectations.
- The product or service you're selling offers a competitive price/value.
- You or your organization have the resources, expertise, and capabilities to deliver what you're promising.
- You will *personally* stand behind your commitments.

Find the Hidden Objections

Any discussion dealing with customer or prospect needs would be incomplete without mentioning hidden objections. Hidden objections are like ice on bridges—unseen and potentially hazardous. For example, a corporate travel planner had several complaints about a particular air carrier's luggage handling from company executives. Salespeople from that airline who call on that travel planner will meet resistance; if they don't probe and if the travel planner is reticent, they may never understand why they aren't being awarded very much business.

Your discovery and probing of needs and desires *must* be thorough. If, during the course of a sales presentation, you have ever found yourself using introductory clauses such as: "Oh, well I assumed that wasn't necessary . . ." or "Gee, I wasn't aware you already had . . ." or "Really? I had no idea you wouldn't purchase . . .", you were victimized by hidden (or maybe not so hidden) objections. Don't forget to probe for hidden objections.

A good way to analyze and understand a customer's or prospect's (audience's) needs is to use a needs analysis chart. You can easily create one on a legal pad. Turn the pad horizontally and rule the page into four columns; then title each column as shown in Figure 2–1: Requirements, Past History, Current Situation, and Desired Fulfillment. Then

FIGURE 2–1

Needs Analysis Grid

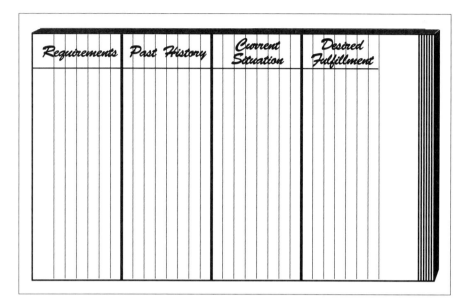

fill it out. If you're not sure that you've identified all the requirements or you cannot articulate the past history, current situation, or desired fulfillment, you've gained important insight—you know what you need to know. Perhaps one or all of your competitors may not be as tenacious as you. But don't count on it.

I don't know about you, but I've never sold against any competitors who told their customers or prospects that they were dedicated to mediocrity, unreliable service, and maximizing profits (the unofficial mission statement of too many business organizations on our planet). Consequently, your ability to *effectively* convince prospects of the verisimilitude of your presentation is critical to winning the business. Enter the power of visual communications.

Knowledge

What do you do if the audience you're presenting to knows quite a lot about your organization? What do you do if they know very little? You may be surprised to learn that your presentation may not vary much in either case. The three most important things an audience wants to know about you and your organization are

1. You have a reasonable understanding of their industry, operations, and the dynamics of their marketplace.

2. You have a solid grasp of their specific needs.

3. You have the wherewithal—experience, resources, talent, track record, commitment—to meet their needs in an optimal fashion.

You should address each of these points early in your presentation. If you're confident the audience you're pitching to has a good understanding of your organization, you should plan to highlight each point. On the other hand, if your audience knows little if anything about you, it's imperative to establish your credibility right away in order to give greater currency to your presentation. Business or marketing videos can do an excellent job of demonstrating your knowledge of a customer's or prospect's business. They also allow you to "show off" (where appropriate) your capital and human resources, unique capabilities, and examples of your work product. Videos also allow you to introduce comments from (satisfied) past and/or current customers. Very powerful. We'll talk about this medium in depth in Chapter 6.

Above all else, you want your audience to trust you and have confidence in your organization. If you fail to create a reasonable degree of trust and confidence, the balance of your presentation will be seriously impaired.

Expertise

Have you ever sat through a presentation where you felt the presenter was talking in a foreign language? I have. Think about this situation from the presenter's point of view for a moment: The presentation objective went unmet, and the audience was alienated. What a waste of time and effort. If this was a sales presentation, I'd sure want to be up against this guy for the business.

If your audience is multidisciplined, be prepared to discuss the features and benefits of your product or service in terms (words, pictures, and concepts) that have a positive impact on each discipline. To illustrate, an industrial-coating salesperson explaining the virtues of a new product to a multidisciplined audience mentions

. . . The beautiful, no-care finish (marketing).

. . . The added product durability (engineering).

. . . The ease of application and cleanup (operations).

. . . The lower cost (finance).

Be prepared to support and expound upon each benefit. If the customer is likely to have a ton of technical questions, smart salespeople know it's best to have a "technical person" with them at the presentation specifically to address those arcane questions.

I'm sure you've heard this advice from day one—if you don't know the answer to a question, don't fake it; respond with "I don't know, but I'll find out and get back to you." Good advice. But frankly, at a sales presentation (which, as you recall, may be your only shot at the business), I'd rather have the expert right next to me. Let my competitor tell them, "I don't know, but I'll find out and get back to you." Who looks smarter?

Audience Analysis Grid

You can use the grid in Figure 2–2 to analyze your audience, enabling you to determine your presentation objective and develop your presentation strategy with greater precision and confidence.

2.4 RULE THREE: DETERMINE YOUR PRESENTATION OBJECTIVE

Once you've qualified your audience, you've amassed enough data and insight to formulate the presentation objective. The operative term here is *presentation objective* (also called a *communications* objective). Your ultimate objective—"selling your ideas" or "winning the business"—is a given.

Determining your objective is the final step you take before you begin to develop your presentation outline—your strategy and tactics. Let's begin by zeroing in on and agreeing to the meaning and use of the terms *objective, strategy,* and *tactic*. Misuse of these terms is rampant throughout the business community, yet the concepts are almost self-defining:

Objective	What you want to achieve.
Strategy	A plan for obtaining your objective.
Tactic	A specific plan element (stratagem).

A simple business case example will further illuminate these definitions:

FIGURE 2–2

Audience Analysis Grid

Content Issue	*Inference*
Needs and Desires – Well understood – Generally understood – Not well-defined	– *Well understood:* Be sure you demonstrate your keen understanding and appreciation of need(s); discuss nuances or subtleties that will help differentiate you from competitors. Be aggressive. – *Generally understood:* Good opportunity for a needs analysis review (chart) to help communicate your understanding of customer's or prospect's need(s). Play to your strengths. – *Not well-defined:* More common in service-driven than in product-driven sales presentations. Usually in these cases the customer or prospect recognizes a problem but cannot clearly define or articulate what it is. This may be a great opportunity to take a risk and try an unconventional approach to win the sale.
Knowledge of Your Company – Very familiar – General – Minimal	– *Very familiar:* May only need to stress any new or significant changes or additions; focus on aspect of organization that directly influences sale (avoid lengthy or canned company overviews—especially if they are of poor quality). – *General:* As above; look for areas to feature that directly relate to how you can meet their needs. – *Minimal:* You must provide an overview of your company—attempt to highlight most relevant aspects but be careful not to overdo the time you spend in this area. If your company has a good overview video, use it; if your company has a good capabilities brochure, distribute copies at the end of your presentation or include them with your written proposal.
Audience Expertise – One discipline – Two or more disciplines	– *One discipline:* The substance and tone of your presentation must be geared to the interests of the discipline in question. – *Two or more disciplines:* Be aware of the needs/desires of all parties with respect to the sale.

Acme International manufactures and markets a line of industrial solvents. It's a highly competitive industry. One of Acme's *objectives* for the fiscal year is to increase market share, in units (barrels), by 4 percent. The *strategy* for obtaining this increased market share is to generate incremental business from current customers. *Tactics* include volume price discounts to customers on sales that exceed prior year

purchases, a sales contest based on increased business from current
____ year-long promotional efforts (direct mail, telemarket-
____ dvertising) targeted to existing customers.

____ der a sales presentation example:

____ Motors saleswoman is making a presentation to a
____ e talking to a decision-making committee represent-
____ nes: engineering, marketing, and manufacturing.
____ y will strongly influence the decision. The prospect is
____ budget restraints, but knows Acme and respects its prod-
reser____ tion *objective* is to convince the audience that Acme's
____ er useful life and a better cost/value relationship
____ competitive motors, including the one the prospect
____ The saleswoman's *strategies* are to (1) demonstrate
____ of superior quality and last longer than competi-
____ and (2) show that the effective cost of her motors is lower
____ of cr____ petitive models, even though the purchase price is
____ *actics* include a brief video demonstrating Acme's
____ ss; the video features the materials Acme uses, its
____ ntrol procedures, patented product features and
____ ials from satisfied users (she especially selected
____ s very positive marketing implications). She will
____ of her product and the products of two leading
____ the one the prospect is currently purchasing) to
____ laims (one of Acme's engineers will attend the
____ for technical support), and she'll have a cost analysis based on
returns, warranty costs, and projected lost sales that support her
lower-effective-cost claim. (I think she's got a great shot at getting this
business if she can believably/powerfully execute her tactics.)

With that clarified, let's consider how you go about determining
your presentation objective. It's a fairly straightforward, two-step
process that actually begins when you qualify your audience:

1. You must *understand* and *address* the needs and desires of
the customer or prospect.

You have to make certain assumptions with respect to the needs
and desires of your client or prospect. Challenge those assumptions.
Are you sure there are no hidden objections? Be sure you truly *understand the nuances* of their needs and desires because your presentation objective must be focused on meeting those needs and desires. To
the extreme, I've had salespeople make "canned" presentations to me
that never came close to meeting my desires. They never took the time
or made the effort to understand my business and how they could
serve me better than my incumbent resources did. Have you ever

made a presentation like that? (I once had a guy 10 minutes into his pitch before we both realized I didn't use or need what he was selling.)

2. You must be sure your objective is provable or quantifiable.

This component is the critical qualifier or measurement of your presentation objective. Presentation objectives that are vague or subjective are difficult to achieve because you are asking the customer or prospect to "take your word for it." Facts and substance rarely lose to hyperbole.

The following objectives are provable:

- ◆ Convince audience we have best after-sale service in the industry.
- ◆ Convince audience we are more experienced with respect to their markets and distribution channels than our competition is.
- ◆ Convince audience that our combination of resources and talent is unmatched by any of our competitors.
- ◆ Convince audience our product will last longer and is more cost effective than any of our competitors' products.

These objectives are subjective:

- ◆ Convince audience we are more committed than our competition is.
- ◆ Convince audience we are more flexible than competitors are.
- ◆ Convince audience we are the best (one of my favorites).

Use the two-step process you just learned to determine your presentation objective. If it doesn't measure up to these criteria, chances are you're not going to make the sale.

2.5 RULE FOUR: DEVELOP YOUR STRATEGIC PRESENTATION OUTLINE

It's impossible for me to find a word or phrase to satisfactorily convey to you the importance of your outline—it's the basis of both the *content* and *visual support* of your presentation. That's why I've termed it *strategic*.

Before we consider the elements of a strategic outline, let's talk about strategic thinking. First of all, there is nothing mystic about strategic thinking—and contrary to conventional wisdom, you don't need an MBA from Harvard or Wharton to be a good strategic thinker.

What you *do* need is the gumption to reject the obvious, trite, same-way-we've-always-done-it, good enough mindset that pervades the business sector and push yourself to consider and try new ideas (see Rule One). Let me give you an example of strategic thinking.

John McLinden worked for years as a project manager for a general contractor. It was a real love–hate job. He *loved* turning raw space and empty buildings into stately offices and gleaming new retail stores. He *hated* the fact that, because he was spread out over so many projects (not to mention working up bids and helping pitch new business), he spent virtually all his time putting out fires and appeasing irate architects, subcontractors and tenants. Figure 2–3 illustrates the traditional organization of a general contracting company and how it would manage your job. As you can see, project sites are run by superintendents (typically tradesmen) who are given the responsibility for a project, but not the authority—a perfect set-up for a worst-case scenario.

John's frustration was shared by many of his peers, evidenced by the high turnover rate most general contractors experienced with project managers. But John had a better idea. He concluded that if project managers handled only one job at a time, they would not only be able to do a better job but also would attain greater job satisfaction.

FIGURE 2–3

Traditional Organization of a General Contracting Company

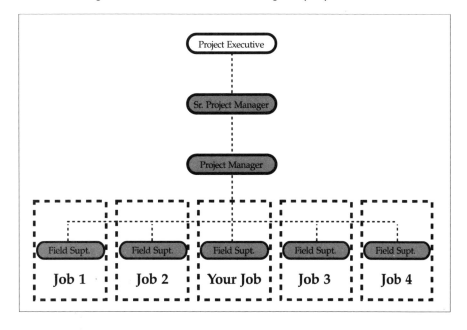

FIGURE 2–4

A "Strategically" Better Idea

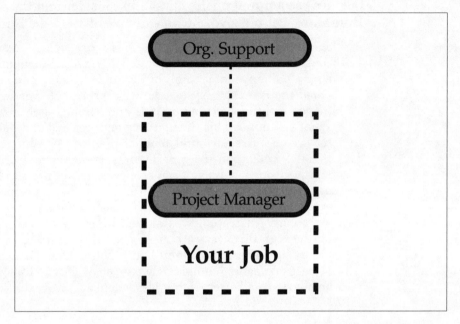

Figure 2–4 illustrates how his organization would handle your job. Elegantly simple isn't it?

John raised the capital, organized the company, hired two project managers, and began to sell his idea. He used a tabletop flip chart to pitch his story of the promise versus the realities of project management and why his firm was the best choice. Even he was amazed at how successful his presentation was; "as soon as I flip that page and reveal our organization, there'd be like a jolt of energy—everyone in the room sits up, you can just feel it."

John's strategic thinking paid off big time. Today, he heads a multi-million-dollar contracting firm and is changing the way many of his competitors do business.

Your Outline Makes a Difference

Now let's relate the concept of strategic thinking to the development of a strategic presentation outline. Every book that I've looked at that deals with the subject of presentations discusses preparation of the outline in the traditional fashion: opening, body, close. This is also known as the tell-them-what-you're-going-to-tell-them; tell-them; and-tell-them-what-you-told-them method. *Let's dare to be different.*

From my experience, I've concluded that six discrete elements comprise a sales presentation:

1. The purpose.
2. Your organization's capabilities and expertise.
3. Your understanding of the customer's or prospect's needs.
4. How you or your organization will meet the customer's or prospect's needs.
5. How you will satisfy the customer's or prospect's desires.
6. Asking for the business.

There is no fixed order or amount of time you need to spend on any one element—remember, your objectives drive your outline. Let's examine these six elements more closely.

1. The Purpose

At some point in the presentation, most often at the onset, it's important to advise your audience of your goals—what you intend to accomplish *today*.

If you think this point is obvious, listen carefully at the next three presentations you attend. I'll wager two of them will not include a stated purpose (and I'll win just about every time). There are three advantages to letting the audience know what you're trying to accomplish:

- ◆ It keeps you focused.
- ◆ It keeps your audience focused (minimizing distractions and extraneous questions).
- ◆ It gives your examples and conclusions more impact.

Sometimes you may not want to state your purpose at the beginning of your presentation. A mood setting vignette; a situational analysis; a diversionary tactic (you may want to "trick" your audience into thinking you're going in one direction and then suddenly veer down an unexpected path for dramatic effect). *Dare to be creative.*

2. Your Capabilities and Expertise

If your audience knows a great deal about you and your company, it's likely you won't need to spend very much time discussing the character, experience, and strengths of your organization. On the other hand, if the audience knows very little about you, it may be necessary to devote a great deal of time to this subject. Audiences that are "mixed" are problematic — you need to cover the topic without boring members of the audience who are familiar with you and your company.

Objectives based on proving an advantage (or advantages) of your organization versus your competitors' would certainly compel you to discuss your company. Your challenge is to present the information in an interesting, meaningful fashion. *Dare to use powerful visuals.*

3. Your Understanding of the Customer's or Prospect's Needs

The key word is *understanding*. When you analyzed the audience (Rule Two), you considered your customer's or prospect's wants and needs. It is critical to the success of the presentation that you clearly communicate to the audience that you understand and appreciate those needs. This can be can be accomplished in a single sentence ("We understand the Acme Lamp Co. needs 5,000 ±20 percent high-quality, 10-inch diameter steel reflectors ready for finishing delivered to its Ohio plant and 5,000 ±20 percent high-quality 12-inch diameter reflectors ready for finishing delivered to its Texas plant by the first Tuesday of each month."), or might require substantial time and detail ("Let's consider the Acme Lamp Co.'s reasons for building a new plant."). In either case, a clear playback of their needs will add credibility to you and your presentation.

Sometimes a customer's or prospect's stated or perceived needs do not agree with their actual needs. In those cases, if you are adroit enough to recognize and correct that misconception, winning the business could be a slam dunk. For example, I've been invited to meet with prospects who tell me they *need* a marketing video or they *need* a capabilities brochure. In those cases, usually the first question I ask them is what they're trying to accomplish. I do that because I want to know their *objective* (recall, that by our definition, a video or brochure is a strategic or tactical consideration—it is *not* an objective). Occasionally, I'll discover that their perceived need will not satisfy their actual need as effectively or efficiently as an alternative strategy. You can imagine their surprise when I come back and present a proposal for a media advertising campaign instead of a brochure. (And I got the business!) *Dare to disagree.*

4. How You Will Meet the Customer's or Prospect's Needs

This element of your presentation should be *process* driven. Wherever possible, number these steps and reinforce your process with visuals. To illustrate this point, let's consider how Acme Metal Stamping might meet the Acme Lamp Co.'s need for reflectors:

> Here's how Acme Metal Stamping will supply you with 5,000 (±20 percent) high-quality, 10-inch diameter steel reflectors ready for finishing delivered to your Ohio plant and 5,000 (± 20 percent) high-quality, 12-inch diameter reflectors ready for finishing delivered to your Texas plant by the first Tuesday of each month:
>
> 1. We will initially inventory 20,000 steel reflectors ready for finishing of each diameter at our Chicago warehouse.
> 2. We will restock our inventory to the 20,000-unit level every 60 days.
> 3. We have primary and alternative carriers (truck and rail) for each market.
> 4. We will schedule shipping for delivery to Ohio and Texas to arrive no later than the last Thursday of each month to a local warehouse.
> 5. Local carriers will deliver to your plants on the first Tuesday of the month.

By presenting how you will meet the customer's needs in this fashion, you simplify complex needs and give basic needs the important consideration they often deserve. You end up looking smart, organized, and thorough. *Dare to think linearly.*

5. How You Will Satisfy the Customer's or Prospect's Desires

Quite often, achieving your objective is determined by how thoroughly and convincingly you satisfy you customer's or prospect's desires. This is usually the time and place to employ the inferences of your strategic thinking. Let's revisit Acme Metal Stamping to illustrate the point of satisfying the *desires* of the Acme Lamp Co.:

◆ Desire 1: High-quality reflectors.

  Heavy-gauge carbon steel used in concert with special dies and presses that are unique to Acme will produce reflectors that are superior in strength and reliability. (Acme should demonstrate or present evidence to support that claim.)

◆ Desire 2: Ready for finishing.

  Acme uses specially formulated, proprietary cleaning and prepping solvents developed in its own lab and maintains rigid quality control standards. This treatment results in superior resistance to corrosion and improved acceptance of all types of finishes. Net effect: better-looking finished prod-uct/fewer rejects. (Acme can show samples; highlight lab.)

♦ Desire 3: Assurance of supply.
Acme has extensive experience in robotic manufacturing, virtually ensuring an uninterrupted labor supply, as well as advanced automated warehousing capabilities to effectively maintain and monitor raw material and finished goods inventories. (Acme should powerfully showcase and prove these advantages.)

♦ Desire 4: Critical importance of on-time delivery.
Acme discussed a redundant delivery procedure from their warehouse utilizing long-distance and local delivery resources. Acme has had positive results with similar pro-grams for several of its customers. (Acme must highlight that experience.)

I believe the point is clear—do whatever it takes to differentiate yourself from your competition to satisfy your customer's or prospect's needs and desires. The tools to *powerfully* communicate your strengths exist:

♦ Videos can show off your resources, manufacturing capabili-ties, and testing procedures as well as feature case studies or testimonials that are both compelling and convincing.

♦ Slides, overhead transparencies, or electronic images will allow you to present and highlight testing reports, man-ufacturing sites, raw material sources, or meeting delivery commitments in a forceful and memorable fashion.

Learn to use these tools. *Dare to be aggressive.*

6. Asking for the Business

The absolute worst thing you can do at a sales presentation is to con-clude it without clearly communicating to your audience what action you expect them to take. Even if they reject your wishes, you have forced them to commit to some future action that gives you a reason to keep the selling process alive. As I've said, there is no fixed order to these elements. I once began a presentation to the Sunbeam Cor-poration by saying, "Gentlemen, after I show you this idea, I fully expect you to award me the project on the spot." I'll tell you more about that presentation later on—it was one of the worst experiences of my life. *Don't you dare forget to ask for the order.*

Preparing Your Outline

How do you begin the development of a strategic presentation outline? The six elements of a presentation are your starting point. Set up a grid or draw a line down the center of a sheet of paper. List the six elements of a presentation on one side and jot down your thoughts and ideas next to each element. These data become the basis for creating your outline and identifying preliminary visual support opportunities. Let's use our pals at Acme Metal Stamping again to illustrate this approach (Figure 2–5).

FIGURE 2–5

Acme's Strategic Presentation Outline Development Grid

Purpose	- Show at meeting how we can <u>guarantee</u> we can meet production and delivery requirements. (4)
Our Capabilities and Expertise	- Important to demonstrate capacity and unique production capabilities. - Show new company video. (1, 2)
Prospect's Needs	- Two sizes of high-quality steel reflectors. - Prepped for finishing (plating). - Must have on-time delivery to two sites. (3, 5)
How We Will Meet Prospect's Needs	- Raw material-production-inventory-delivery-plan, cost/terms. (7, 8)
How We Will Satisfy Prospect's Desires	- Raw material sourcing. - Automation. - Custom dies. - Special prepping solvent. - Inventory control. - Redundant delivery system (experience with current customers). (2, 6, 7)
Ask For Business	- Stress need to begin at once in order to meet their market demand requirements. (9)

Now, using our grid, we can develop a presentation outline for Acme Metal Stamping:

1. Welcome audience.
   - Thank for opportunity to earn their business.
   - Overview how presentation will flow; invite them to ask questions.
   - Open with point that since many may not be familiar with our company, want to introduce them to our experience and capabilities.
2. Present company capabilities and expertise (video).
3. Cover prospect's complete requirement for reflectors (specifications and delivery).
4. Position that we are here today to present how we will meet their requirements—guaranteed!
5. Underscore critical needs: assurance of supply, quality, on-time delivery.
6. Highlight key issues relative to above requirements.
   - Show Baldrige Award mention for QC program.
   - Provide examples of steel we'd produce from and note *four* supply sources (map) from which we can obtain this grade of steel on a two-day delivery basis if ever required (samples).
   - Discuss proprietary solvents and coatings—tell the why we create-our-own story (consider having head of facility make presentation if time permits; pass out "comparison" samples).
7. Outline our methodology and procedures for production, finishing, inventory, and delivery.
   - Present case studies of two customers for whom we have set up similar delivery arrangements (show testimonial letters from those customers).
8. Present cost data (discuss payment terms).
9. Advise prospects they can have first shipment 90 days after they give us the go-ahead (use calendar to show how giving us the go-ahead today will give them the edge they need to have inventory to meet their projected demand).

Did you pinpoint the six elements of a presentation? I hope so; it's much easier than finding Waldo. (Hint: The numbers in the grid of Figure 2–5 refer to the preceding outline.)

2.6 RULE FIVE: ELABORATE CONTENT

Unless you're writing a full-blown script for a tightly structured formal presentation, you will *not* be expanding your outline into a narrative. In fact, unless you're planning to read your presentation (and I can't imagine why you would unless it was for the reason I just cited) *do not expand your outline into a narrative*—you will absolutely kill yourself trying to remember what you wrote. (Mensa members with photographic memories excepted.)

Nevertheless, preparing an effective presentation requires you to perform various tasks or to take actions which allow you to meet the needs and desires of your customer or prospect. You may need to consider:

- Pricing
- Competitive analyses
- Staffing
- Market research
- Prototype development
- Materials procurement
- Concept development
- Coalescing of samples
- System design
- Photography/videography
- Et cetera

Whether you have just a few unresolved issues or so many you're overwhelmed, there is a preferred way to expand upon your outline. The procedure I am going to suggest you follow is rather straightforward. It may at first appear rather formal or even redundant, but after you've followed it a few times, you'll see it's fast, efficient, and comprehensive:

1. Establish a *communications objective* for each point. Specifically, determine what you want the audience to take away from each segment of your presentation.

2. Identify those points you need to develop more fully (what you need to know and what actions to take) and which points meet *desires*.

3. Address those points that need further development. Make every effort to accomplish those tasks in a timely fashion so

you'll have enough time to properly prepare, rehearse, and stage your presentation.

4. Give special attention to points you've identified as meeting customer or prospect *desires.* You'll want to emphasize those points using the *language of visual communications* to its best advantage.

Evaluate as You Elaborate

I don't believe it's necessary for me to spend a great deal of time discussing *how* to elaborate. In truth, I'm not even sure how to go about that. But what I can do is provide you with a simple, effective means of *evaluating* your content. Shallow, insipid, unimaginative, off-target content can cost you a sale. No discussion.

Many years ago I attended an Association of National Advertisers (ANA) seminar on creative advertising. One of the lecturers presented guidelines for evaluating creative submissions, covering a broad array of categories. It was an impressive presentation (yes, with visuals). More than 20 years have passed since I attended that seminar, and I am still using what I learned (albeit with some slight modifications) to check my work. Here are the four questions you must answer yes to when evaluating sales presentation content:

1. Meaningful/*unique*
   Is my presentation relevant to members of the audience and have I addressed their needs in an interesting fashion?

2. Credible/*persuasive*
   Will the audience believe what I'm saying—are my conclusions valid and meaningful?

3. Motivating/*forceful*
   Are my arguments capable of compelling my audience to take action?

4. Memorable/*distinctive*
   Have I done everything possible to make *my* presentation the standard by which all others will be measured?

Without the trappings of the seminar and the eloquence of the presenter, these evaluation guidelines may seem pedestrian—but please don't dismiss them out of hand. Think about these four questions in the context of presentations you've heard or given yourself.

If the content measured up to these criteria, somebody was probably making a sale. I suggest you write down these questions and put them in a prominent place where you can refer to them often until they become *de rigueur* with every sales presentation you make.

Now you're ready to begin storyboarding. Your storyboard is an evolving, indispensable tool that helps you build a powerful presentation. It's for those reasons that you begin to storyboard even before all your content has been developed. Let me show you why.

2.7 RULE SIX: CREATE A PRESENTATION STORYBOARD

Don't panic. Storyboarding is not about art; it's about conceptual thinking. Storyboards are visualizations of your outline—chronological representations of the words, symbols, images, charts and graphs you intend to use to visually support your presentation. *Visualizing* your outline is important because it compels you to organize your thoughts more cogently; it forces you to shape your presentation more exactly and to develop your arguments more forcefully. A storyboard will help you see where your presentation is lacking substance or support and make it easier for you to identify and correct those shortcomings.

For these reasons and more, storyboards are essential to the development of powerful business presentations. Yet from my experience, very few business professionals create storyboards to help them organize their presentations. Perhaps no one ever told them it was a good idea, or maybe they believe they need to be artistic to create one (a conclusion that couldn't be more wrong as you'll see from *my* examples in this book—no one will ever confuse me with Claude Monet).

Always create a storyboard. Regardless of how simple or complex your presentation is going to be, a storyboard will improve its flow and content.

The Storyboard Formats of Choice

Over the years I have created and used 14 different storyboard formats. However, I use two configurations about 95 percent of the time: a four-by-six horizontal grid (Figure 2–6) and a two-by-six vertical grid (Figure 2–7), which I'll talk about in Rule 7.

Storyboard formats are easy to make on a computer or by hand using an 8½-by-11-inch sheet of plain white paper. After you've made

F I G U R E   2–6

4 x 6 Horizontal Grid

your master, you can make a zillion copies on any standard office copier. Use a pencil that has an eraser to draft your storyboard. And remember, *storyboarding has nothing to do with art;* it's a tool to help you manage and improve presentation content and flow.

F I G U R E 2–7

2 x 6 Vertical Grid

Using a four-by-six storyboard format, let's create a storyboard from the strategic outline we developed for Acme Metal Stamping's presentation to the Acme Lamp Co. This time, consistent with the Rules of Power Pitching, I'll add the communications objective for each point.

1. Welcome audience.
   - Thank them for opportunity to earn their business.
   - Overview how presentation will flow; invite them to ask questions.
   - Open with point that since many may not be familiar with company, want to introduce them to our experience and capabilities.

   Communications Objective: *establish structure and set tone*

2. Present company capabilities and expertise (video).

   Communications Objective: *impress audience with company's sophistication, scope, experience, and strengths*

3. Cover prospect's complete requirement for reflectors (specifications and delivery).

   Communications Objective: *demonstrate understanding of needs*

4. Position that we are here today to present how we will meet their requirements—guaranteed!

   Communications Objective: *exhibit confidence in abilities*

5. Underscore critical needs: assurance of supply, quality, on-time delivery.

   Communications Objective: *reinforce grasp of needs and desires*

6. Highlight key issues relative to above requirements.
   - Show Baldrige Award mention for QC program.
   - Provide examples of steel we'd produce from and note *four* supply sources (map) from which we can obtain this grade of steel on a two-day delivery basis if ever required (samples).
   - Discuss proprietary solvents and coatings—tell them why we create-our-own story (consider having head of facility make presentation if time permits; pass out "comparison" samples).
   - Present case studies of two customers for whom we have set up similar delivery arrangements (show testimonial letters from those customers).

Communications Objective: *create positive net impression of our strengths and capabilities vis-a-vis desires*

7. Outline our methodology and procedures for production, prepping for finishing, inventory, and delivery.

Communications Objective: *demonstrate problem-solving abilities/competence*

8. Present pricing data (discuss payment terms).

Communications Objective: *responsiveness/competitiveness*

9. Advise prospects they can have first shipment 90 days after they give us the go-ahead (use calendar to show how giving us the go-ahead today will give them the edge they need to have inventory to meet their projected demand).

Communications Objective: *create urgency*

Figure 2–8 is the storyboard I developed using Acme Metal Stamping's strategic outline. You'll note that I plan to have a title to my presentation, Meeting Your Needs (OK it's hokey, but I'm just trying to make a point, so lighten up). You can easily see my preliminary visual support ideas (video, map, photos, charts, and graphs, some of which I had already considered in the outline). I hope you also noticed that I didn't *literally* follow the strategic outline (recall that I said storyboarding helps you identify shortcomings and gives you the opportunity to remedy them, and that's just what I did).

Notable variances: In addition to expanding several points, I moved the case studies citing Acme Metal Stamping's ability to meet demanding delivery schedules to a more strategic position—supporting the proposed delivery plan. I also augmented my presentation of cost data to include a second option using a slightly higher gauge of steel in case price became a serious issue. These thoughts (improvements) came to me as I created the storyboard. Can you suggest other changes? If you can, then you're beginning to get the hang of it—keep it up.

There is another virtue to storyboarding that pays handsome dividends. Because the responsibility for creating *finished* visuals is typically outsourced or managed by in-house creative/marketing service personnel or departments, your storyboard will be especially useful in helping them create *powerful finished* visuals. Creative people love storyboards.

FIGURE 2-8

Storyboard for Acme Metal Stamping

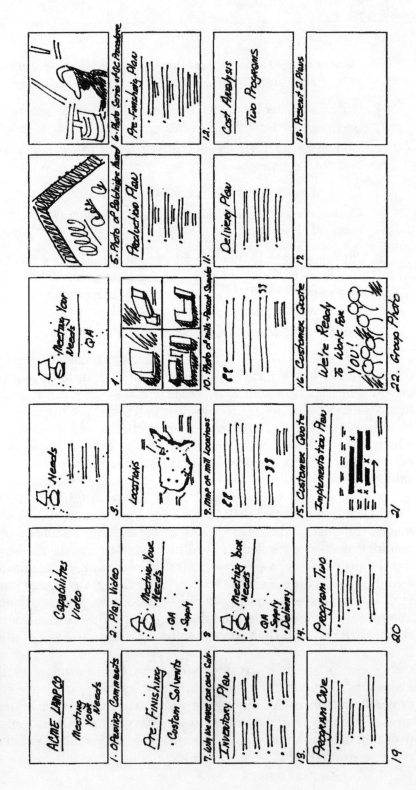

Are you becoming more convinced about the benefits of story-boarding? As you become more practiced at it, you'll find that not only will your presentations be more powerful, but you'll dramatically reduce the amount of time it takes you to organize and prepare your presentations.

Now let's examine how from little storyboards mighty presentations grow.

2.8 RULE SEVEN: USE VISUALS TO SIMPLIFY AND AMPLIFY KEY POINTS

Simplification and amplification are techniques that help you create more powerful presentation visuals. Please believe me when I say it's far more important for you to *comprehend* the concepts of visual simplification and amplification than it is for you to be able to execute them. As I just noted, you are most often not personally responsible for creating finished visuals. As such, concomitant with understanding concepts of simplification and amplification, you need to have the ability to provide your creative resources with lucid, intelligent direction. This book will help you develop your ability to effectively direct and motivate creative resources.

Simplification

Simplification is a visual communications technique. The *object* of simplification is to express your ideas, insights, polemics, recommendations, conclusions, and so on with greater precision and impact. The *result* (and benefit) of this goal is a highly memorable presentation. Simplification helps keep the audience's attention on you by agreeing with and underscoring *what you are telling them.* Visuals that are too wordy, too obtuse, or require the audience to perform calculations, can be highly distracting and cause you to lose your audience. Your point may not be made, or worse, completely misunderstood.

Visual simplification is usually a matter of supplanting text with symbols or imagery; sometimes simplification is subtractive (reducing the amount of text and/or adding emphasis to text). The simplification process begins with your strategic outline, more specifically with your communications objectives (your communications objectives should drive your visuals). Let's compare and discuss visual support alternatives.

FIGURE 2-9

Emphasizing Key Points

We Will Maintain Both Raw Materials and Finished Goods Inventory Levels at 120 Days	120 Days Inventory • Raw Materials • Finished Goods

Communications Objective: Demonstrate Commitment to Inventory Support

Figure 2-9 illustrates how text can be pared down and emphasis directed to a benefit. If long-term inventory support is key, which of the above visuals makes that point more effectively—more memorably? Avoid visuals that merely parrot what you say; eventually the audience will tune them out (and you with them). Let your visuals underscore and bring to life your key points.

Communications Objective: Impress Audience with Long-Term Growth History

Figure 2-10 is a typical translation of data (text) to chart form. The bar chart *instantly* makes the point of long-term growth history, whereas the columns of dates and numbers force the audience to read the data and perform the necessary calculations to support your claim. I haven't seen many sales presentations that didn't include at least a few charts and graphs. Consequently, easily understood, well-

FIGURE 2-10

Translation of Data to Chart

ACME Sales & Profit Trends (1992-1999)		
Year	**Sales**	**Net Profit**
1992	531,000	20,158,000
1993	625,000	23,165,000
1994	730,000	29,600,000
1995	860,000	40,900,000
1996	843,000	22,100,000
1997	966,000	36,700,000
1998	1,111,000	51,365,000
1999	1,290,000	57,550,000

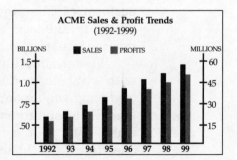

Source: S.O.S., Chicago. Used with permission.

FIGURE 2–11

Adding Credibility to "Delivery-in-24 Hours"

ACME U.S. LOCATIONS by REGION		
EAST	**CENTRAL**	**WEST**
N.Y.C.	Chicago	L.A.
Boston	St. Louis	Seattle
Philadelphia	Detroit	Dallas
Atlanta	Cleveland	Denver
Miami	Pittsburgh	Portland
Baltimore	Little Rock	Boise
Tampa		

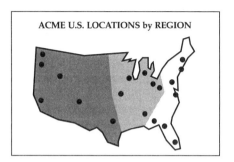

ACME U.S. LOCATIONS by REGION

Source: S.O.S., Chicago. Used with permission.

produced charts and graphs are integral to Power Pitching. I'll be reviewing the very important subject of basic chart and graph design and presentation in Chapter 3.

Communications Objective: Ability to Deliver Anywhere in the United States in 24 hours

Figure 2–11 employs a map (a symbol) that adds *credibility* and memorability to your delivery-in-24-hours claim. Maps are an important and widely used simplification tool.

Communications Objective: Show High-Tech Manufacturing Capabilities

"If you got it, flaunt it," the old ad slogan exhorts. Well conceived photo images are incredibly powerful. Not only do they often add credibility and memorability to your presentation, they can be extremely motivational in and of themselves ("I want to see *that* for myself!"; "I want our packaging to look like that!"; "I can't believe they were able to do that in only 20 square feet—I'm impressed!"). Figure 2–12 gives me confidence in that manufacturer's ability to deliver on its promises.

Communications Objective: Impress with Attention to Detail

Here we've *added* visuals to simplify. The large plan drawing with all the callouts and minutia (Figure 2–13) is classic information overload. The audience in all likelihood can't read all the small print or clearly see the detail you're alluding to. By presenting a series of visuals below, the audience plainly sees, and can better appreciate, each detail you're discussing. Your point is made even stronger by the repetition of the visuals—you're saying, "we pay attention to details"

FIGURE 2–12

Photographs Make the Point

© Michael Rosenfeld/Tony Stone Images. Used with permission.

again and again and again. This example of simplification overlaps the technique of amplification, which we'll talk about next, and introduces the concept of visual impressions, which will be covered in Rule 8.

Amplification

Amplification is a positioning technique. The object of amplification is to firmly *position* you or your organization as possessing knowledge, products, experience, talent, or other attributes that distinguish you from your competition. Once again your communications objectives will give you direction by helping you determine where to place emphasis—what needs or desires to emphatically address. Your customer or prospect may desire to have a resource with a national service organization or a history of working with new product introductions or experience in handling real estate requirements for law firms or a "business partner" with special insights and knowledge of the market. If that's the case, you want to be sure your credentials are powerfully presented to that audience.

Back in the early 80s, Abbott Laboratories HomeCare group was a late entry into the rapidly growing home health care marketplace; its mission was to be a provider of home health care services. For a myriad of reasons the business wasn't making plan, not least among them was a sales force that was more comfortable selling products and science than services. After much consideration and debate, a new strategy to grow the home care market was adopted. The thrust

FIGURE 2–13

Complex Floor Plan versus Details of Plan

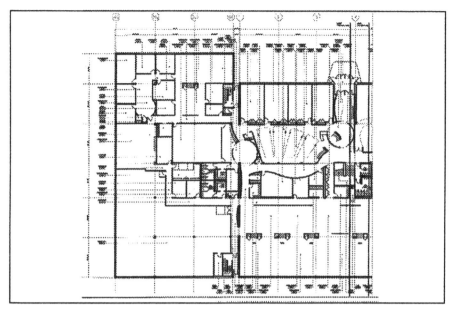

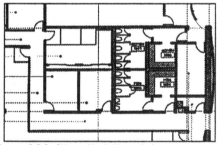 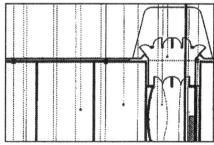

Source: S.O.S., Chicago. Used with permission.

of the strategy was to form "partnerships" with hospitals to help *them* successfully enter the home care market. One of the key sales presentation tools, used by Abbott sales reps responsible for selling the partnership concept, was a 10-minute video that discussed the tremendous pressure the health care/hospital sector was attempting to deal with and the principal reasons behind this pressure. The video opened with news footage of LBJ signing the Medicare Bill in 1965 and concluded by pointing out that home health care was an option for hospitals to help generate incremental revenue and maintain patients. The communications objective of the video was to position Abbott's Home-Care group as having a profound understanding of the problems most hospitals were dealing with and a viable strategy to help ameliorate those problems. The video helped many of the reps overcome their anxieties about selling a concept; they found their customers were eager to talk to someone who both understood and offered a solution to their problems. (Today, HomeCare is one of Abbott's most profitable business units.)

I like to think of *amplification* as being a mini-presentation(s) within the sales presentation—vignettes devoted to helping achieve the presentation objective. Amplifying with case histories, testimonials, historical retrospectives, visual tours, comparative analyses, or testing procedures and results, for example, can often be the highlight (the most memorable aspect) of your sales presentation.

A Look at the Two-by-Four Vertical Storyboard Format

Because of its larger size, I like to use the two-by-four vertical storyboard format for simplifying or amplifying. If you wish, you can redo your entire storyboard on this format; you can redraft specific visuals that may require more detail to allow them to be effectively reproduced, or you can call out and create mini-presentations. Figure 2–14 and Figure 2–15 show how I detailed two specific visuals and crafted a mini-presentation for Acme Metal Stamping's presentation to the Acme Lamp Co. Be aware that each time you transfer (and expand) your outline to a storyboard, your presentation grows stronger.

When all your storyboarding is complete, you can begin to plan the staging of your presentation and the production of your visual support.

2.9 RULE EIGHT: PLAN THE MEDIA SELECTION, DELIVERY, AND STAGING OF YOUR PRESENTATION

With the substance of your presentation well in hand, and before you begin the process of creating visuals, you need to concern yourself with the mundane but nonetheless momentous matter of presentation media selection, delivery, and staging. Don't minimize the importance of staging. Think about the difference between a Broadway production of *Phantom of the Opera* and your local high school's version—you expect professionalism and sophistication from a Broadway musical; in a high school production you're happy if your kid doesn't fall off the stage. Most customers and prospects *expect* (and prefer) professionalism and sophistication from their resources.

FIGURE 2–14

Storyboard 1

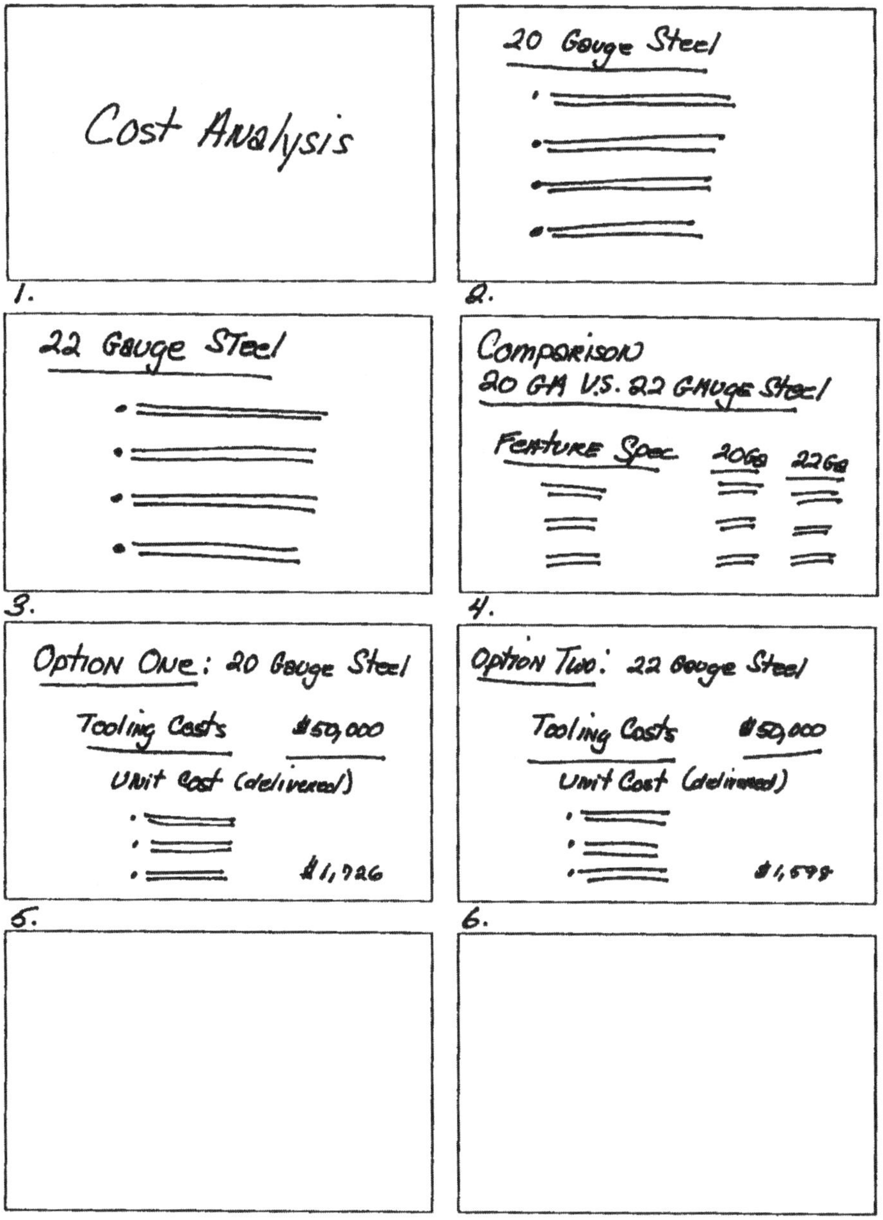

F I G U R E 2–15

Storyboard 2

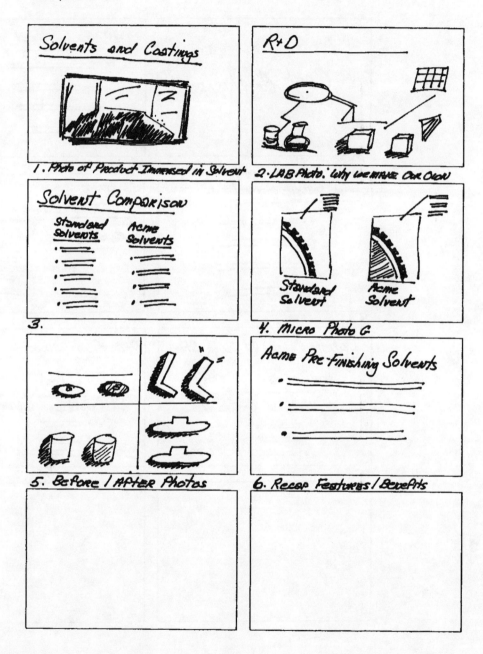

Don't Fall off the Stage

The planning begins with an analysis of fundamental presentation constraints and characteristics:

1. How large is the audience you'll be presenting to?
2. Where will the presentation be made?
3. How much time do you have to make the presentation?

Following this review, you'll know which medium or media will best manifest your message. The review must be comprehensive.

◆ Audience size: How large is the audience?

Audience size will range from one-on-one presentations between you and a decision maker (ideal) all the way to megameetings with a decision-making committee replete with interested influencers (problematic). Unfortunately, you rarely have much control over this variable.

Generally, small meetings allow you more flexibility: you can keep your meeting more loosely structured, more intimate. As I mentioned earlier, I prefer this style because you generally have greater control—you have the flexibility to switch gears if you sense unanticipated feedback (positive or negative) from the audience. You can be more yourself in this type of meeting, which means the tone of the meeting will be more comfortable for you.

Larger scale meetings tend to take on more structure and may require more sophisticated visual support (e.g., slides or projected electronic images). This is not necessarily all bad, regardless of whether you're the favorite or a dark horse to win the business. If you can distinguish your presentation from competition with thoughtful, relevant substance and powerful visuals, you can often win in a landslide (as expected) or pull off a major upset.

To repeat, the smaller the audience the better. Sales presentations to larger audiences typically have more unknowns. (You may also need to invite "experts," for example, an engineer, designer, or programmer to participate in the presentation directly or be available to answer technical questions—another variable that can spin you out of control.)

◆ Presentation venue: Is the meeting at your office, their office, or at a neutral site?

If you have control over this variable you again need to refer to your objective. If showing off your resources and capabilities is important to your presentation, a plant or office tour may be exactly what you desire. On the other hand, if you feel your plant or office may not "show" as well as most of your competitors, you might be better off on your customer's or prospect's turf, using videos or slides to conduct your "tour."

I'm probably in the minority here, but I prefer pitching on the road. When I'm on the road, I tend to be less distracted by home office people and events and I'm generally better rehearsed. The playing field seems to be leveler (at least that's my perception). But being successful on the road demands being well prepared. If you're at a customer's or prospect's location or at a neutral site, you need to know if any restrictions or conditions may impact the delivery of your presentation. Be sure the *means* of projecting or displaying your presentation support is available to you—if not, you'll need to make alternative plans, so be sure to determine if space, electrical power, lighting controls, etc. are adequate (please do that in a timely fashion). And if at all possible, try to rehearse at the unfamiliar site— especially if you are using audiovisual support.

I once staged a slide presentation in Florida where the humidity was so intense that moisture penetrated the glass mounted slides. When the slides were projected, the moisture was energized by the heat of the projection lamp—it appeared to the audience that microscopic life forms were attacking the images on the screen—very distracting. After that experience, I never staged a sales meeting in Florida again without *two* blow driers and a backup set of glassless mounted slides in my briefcase.

A neutral site implies your customer or prospect will likely be seeing several presentations in a short time frame. If possible, try to be *first*. ("What?!" you probably just said to yourself, "I've always heard it's better to be last.") From my experience, being first, last, or in the middle doesn't usually matter all that much if your presentation is crammed with interesting facts and good ideas. But I like going first at neutral site because these meetings are usually all business—the audience wants to hear the presentations and get back home ASAP. So if you follow the Ten Rules of Power Pitching and make a powerful lead-off presentation, you've now set a standard that others must, at the very least, come up to. If they can't, the audience will quickly turn them off. Think about that.

♦ Time allocation: Is there a time constraint, or do you have as much time as you want/need?

Just like a football game, the clock can be your best friend or your worst enemy. Frankly, I like time limits. If you're smart (prepared), you'll have distilled the presentation down to its essence, trimmed the fat, properly rehearsed, and stand ready to deliver a cogent presentation supported by powerful visuals (which is exactly what you should be doing under any circumstance). Frankly, you'll be tough to beat.

Conversely, time limits kill people who are unprepared. They will invariably commit the three deadly sales presenter sins:

1. They will devote most of their time covering the topic (or topics) they know best and gloss over others (which may be the crucial ones).

2. They will allow distractions and questions to sidetrack them.

3. They will wind up rushing to their denouement.

Make time your friend. If you are under a tight time constraint, be sure you can cover all the material in the allotted time by clocking your rehearsals. Make adjustments if necessary and be sure to allow room for unexpected questions or interruptions. Great visuals are great time savers. As you know, you can simplify complex or abstract ideas with a few well-conceived charts, photographs, or illustrations (Rule 7). If your audience gets tripped up over an unreadable chart or a series of confusing images, you'll be wasting precious minutes trying to "unconfuse" them (and you may not be successful).

Media Selection and Staging

After considering your strategic outline (content) plus audience size, venue, and time (logistics), your presentation medium practically selects itself. Figure 2–16 is a useful tool with additional insights to help you choose the proper presentation medium (or media) and design the staging of your presentation:

Presentation Delivery

Finally, you need to determine how you intend to deliver your presentation. You have limited options:

1. Read from a script cuing visuals (only for very tightly structured presentations).

2. Use notes and visuals.

3. Let your visuals lead you.

FIGURE 2–16

Presentation Media/Staging Guidelines

Logistic Issue	*Inference*

Audience Size
  – One on one
  – Two to five
  – More than five
	– *One on one:* Loosely structured; informal tone if well acquainted with customer or prospect; keep visual support "simple" (passouts or overhead transparencies, video if appropriate); aggressively address satisfying desires. Also optimal size for laptop multimedia presentation.
	– *Two to five:* As above; tone may be more formal if you are not well acquainted with all members of audience; all media can work here, but try to avoid slides if at all possible (you lose intimacy).
	– *More than five:* Probably have to tighten structure, especially if more than one discipline in audience; be sure visuals of proper size (everyone in the room should be able to read or understand visuals).

Presentation Venue
  – Home site
  – Customer/prospect site
  – Neutral site
	– *Home site:* Be sure everyone at your company knows a customer or prospect will be visiting you (give ample warning and send a reminder notice the day before). Have presentation location and any areas they may visit looking sharp. Do all you can to make visitors feel welcome, comfortable, and *important* (provide an office, phone, fax, modem, etc. if possible/desirable). On your home ground, confidence should exude from your presentation.
	– *Customer/prospect site:* Be on time; if rehearsal or setup of audiovisual equipment is necessary, try to arrange (well in advance) to get into presentation venue early (the night before would be satisfactory). If you are following another presentation, you will generally have time to set up for your pitch—do a trial run to be sure you can accomplish your setup in the allotted time.
	– *Neutral site:* As above; if there are several presentations that day, try to be the first. If at all possible try to arrive a day early so you can scout the location and identify (and solve) any problems that might adversely affect your presentation.

Time
  – No limit
  – Limited
	– *No limit:* Be careful of information overloaditis, ignore minutia; in fact, sometimes a brief presentation will allow you to stand out from your competitors. You may also be tempted to include everyone who is involved in the delivery of the product or service in the presentation—don't.
	– *Limited:* You must be well rehearsed; if you are using audiovisual support, be sure the equipment works flawlessly. Tighter structure is likely desirable, especially if your allocated time is severely limited; be sure your visual support is well conceived or it's going to be a long plane ride home.

For most of you, the number of times you will make a sales presentation reading from a script will be equal to the number of times you'll win the lottery. You will almost always present from notes or use your visuals to guide you through your presentation. The differences between the two are subtle. When you use notes, your commentary generally *sets up* a visual to conclude, clarify, or make a point. When you use visuals as prompts, you refer to the text, symbol, or imagery of the visual—again to reach a conclusion, clarify, or make a point. Your decision to use notes or to speak extemporaneously is a matter of

1. Your rehearsal (did you have enough run throughs and did they go well?).
2. The complexity of the data you're presenting.
3. Your comfort level (both with the material you're covering and with the notion of flying without a safety net).

Many experts believe you make a better impression on the audience if you speak without notes. I'm not in total agreement with that point of view when it comes to giving sales presentations. You may look too slick, too polished—as if you've memorized the presentation without really being invested (sincere or knowledgeable) in what you are saying. Even if you've made this pitch a thousand times, you need to make it appear as if it's new and fresh—that you put it together expressly for this particular customer or prospect. Make your audience feel important. Make them feel special.

Humor Me—Use Humor with Care

Humor is tricky in sales presentations. It often falls flat (bad enough) or occasionally offends someone (deadly). My advice is to be very conservative in your use of humor. Here are my views on the subject:

- I think humor has a place in most presentations, it's an effective way to develop rapport with an audience—especially if there are people in that audience with whom you're not familiar—but it must be in good taste. (Warning: taste is very subjective.)
- If you think there is even the slightest chance you may offend someone with a joke, story, or barb, hit the delete key at once.

- I am personally not fond of telling jokes unless I wish to make a specific point or the joke has a direct tie-in to the presentation (even in those cases I'd look for a less predictable lead-in). True or apocryphal anecdotes are more interesting; plus I think they make you look more intelligent and better prepared. Anybody (except my wife) can tell a joke.

- *Do not make yourself look foolish.* Self-deprecation is not acceptable.

- As a corollary to the above: Do not poke fun at anyone in the audience, even if you know everyone well. OK, I suppose if you went out socially the evening before your presentation and had a real blast you might make some reference to a particularly humorous episode. Just be sensitive to what you say and who you pick on. (If your boss is with you, pick on him or her; play it safe.)

I once hired a piano bar comedian to perform after dinner at a sales meeting we were producing for Eli Lilly and Company. The meeting was for a small number of senior managers (all male). The dinner was being held at the top of the tallest building in Indianapolis (at least it was at the time) in a private club that many of the Lilly brass belonged to and frequented. My contact at Lilly, Bill Wheeler was a very bright, very likable, top-gun marketer. He also knew his way around Lilly's politics. He had warned me that *my* comedian better keep his material sanitized. I obeyed and warned *my* comedian to keep his act clean. "Not a problem, I'm a pro," he reassured me. The after dinner show began splendidly. Cocktails were served, and the piano bar comedian sang and told some uproarious stories. Bill was pleased. Then one of the managers asked if he could tell a joke. "Go Frank!" howled the crowd. That did it. The jokes got bluer and bluer (with *my* comedian doing more than holding his own). I figured, what the heck, they started it; and everyone, including me, was on the floor laughing. Then I noticed Bill was gone. About two minutes later a maitre d' type came into our private room and told me I had a telephone call. It was Bill. "End that party and get them out of there now." Click. I froze. In an instant I realized I had failed to meet my professional responsibility to my client. I had allowed a business meeting to turn into a stag party. I zoomed back to the room and immediately ended the party to the protestations and derisive groans of the managers. Thankfully, Bill was forgiving and didn't fire me on the spot. In fact, we continued to work together for many years and are still good friends. Funny how things turn out.

Presentation Connotation

As I've mentioned several times, you can lose business by being unprepared, unsophisticated, or uncommitted. And if I may be blunt, being uncommitted, unprepared, or unsophisticated is easily communicated to your audience.

Shortly after I started writing this book I attended a presentation sponsored by a multimedia company discussing the Internet and home pages. It was part of a larger conference dealing with new-age marketing communications tools. Here's a recap of what I experienced at that presentation:

1. The room the presentation was to be held in was misposted on the conference agenda, so people who came specifically to witness this presentation had to search for it.

2. The meeting, which had a 90-minute time frame, started late (for obvious reasons).

3. While waiting for latecomers, the two speakers (the president of the company and the vice president of sales) stood around the podium joking and talking to each other, generally ignoring the people in the audience. (They also seemed to ignore fact that no one knew where their presentation was being held.)

4. The opening speaker was the vice president of sales; his microphone initially failed to work.

5. Visuals were projected on a standard audiovisual screen using a laptop computer and an LCD projector. Unfortunately, nobody bothered to turn down the lights until about half way through the opening speaker's remarks, so the visuals weren't readable. No one in the audience—including me!—complained about not being able to see the visuals. (This is not as unusual as you might think; consider the number of times you've sat in the back of a room and couldn't hear the speaker. More often than not, I'll bet you sat mute.)

6. The president spoke with his hands in his pockets looking down at the floor most of the time and seemed uncomfortable (unrehearsed). His comments were disjointed.

7. Their live Internet demo failed to work—they were unable to get on-line and had no backup, so they talked us through it.

8. They ran out of time (surprise!), preventing them from answering the questions of the information-starved audience. But they were able to pass out their business cards.

I would like to tell you that I made up this story to make my point, but I would be lying. What makes this tale especially sorrowful—but relevant—is that this presentation was a significant new business opportunity for this company. What they had to say was timely, interesting, and meaningful. (The visuals were terrific once you could see them.) But would you hire these guys to be your multimedia or Internet resource? I don't think so. Their presentation *connoted* lack of planning, lack of attention to detail, lack of professionalism, and lack of commitment. As I said, easy to do.

Don't Fall off the Stage—Part II

Would you make a sales presentation in sweaty workout clothes? With your hair uncombed? After eating a gyros? Not likely. You want to make a good impression on your customer or prospect. So what would your customer or prospect think of you if

+ You turn on a slide projector and the slide is projected backwards, or it's dirty or out of sequence?
+ Your presentation board is dog-eared?
+ Your overhead transparency has obvious spelling and/or grammar errors?
+ Your video starts in the middle or fails to work?

You'd probably have been better off eating a gyros.

2.10 RULE NINE: PRODUCE YOUR PRESENTATION VISUALS IN A MANNER CONSISTENT WITH YOUR PRESENTATION OBJECTIVE AND STRATEGY

I mentioned earlier that the responsibility for creating *finished* visuals is usually outsourced or handled by in-house creative services. By following the rules of power pitching you are now able to provide those resources with the type of information and direction required to create powerful visuals. In addition to your rough storyboards, you can clearly articulate your presentation's objective, style, tone, audience characteristics, and staging plans. Remember, creative people love detailed input—it makes their jobs easier and more satisfying. Trust me, they will absolutely love you for doing this. Their love will be manifested in the quality of their output.

In subsequent chapters I'm going to give you general guidelines for the creation of visuals. These guidelines will further help you direct—and even more importantly—evaluate creative output to ensure you are armed and ready to make powerful, winning business presentations.

2.11 RULE TEN: REHEARSE, REHEARSE

I can tell you unequivocally that all your hard work, your great ideas, and your powerful visuals can be rendered impotent if you don't rehearse your presentation.

Rehearsing Is Never Having to Say "Oops"

Rehearsing doesn't mean reading through your notes in the parking lot 15 minutes before meeting with your customer or prospect. Rehearsing means delivering your presentation under conditions as close to the real thing as possible—having an audience present, using your visuals, answering questions, planning for contingencies. I even used to rehearse what to do if a slide projector bulb blew or an errant visual appeared. It also means that if you're presenting as a group, *rehearse as a group.* If you are planning to have one or more associates at the presentation to answer questions or otherwise participate, it would be valuable to have that person or those people present while you rehearse. They will have a better understanding of their roles and responsibilities as well as becoming aware of the issues you'll be addressing. (If having them at the rehearsal isn't possible, at the very least you must review your presentation with them and acquaint them to the possible problems or questions they may be required to address.)

Rehearsal 101

The following are what I consider to be rehearsal fundamentals:

1. Leave yourself enough time to rehearse properly. In most cases you'll only need a few hours the day before you make the presentation.

The more structured the presentation, the more time you'll require; very elaborate audiovisual presentations sometimes require several *days* of rehearsal.

2. Plan on a minimum of *three* run-throughs. Your initial run-through should be for continuity—you want to be sure your presentation makes sense. If it doesn't, fix it at once. Subsequent run-throughs will help you get comfortable using your visuals in the manner for which you intended them—to clarify, underscore, support or conclude. Don't worry about overrehearsing. You'll know when you've reached your comfort level. Audiences interpret comfort as *confidence*.

3. Rehearse with any notes you plan on using and be sure to use the *same notes* when you give the presentation.

4. Be aware of those places in the presentation where you anticipate or intend to solicit questions from your audience. Make a comprehensive list of probable questions and rehearse your responses.

5. Familiarize yourself with your visuals, especially charts, tables, factoids, and the like. Be prepared for unexpected conclusions, inferences, or challenges to your data. If you can't back up a fact or claim, lose it.

6. Rehearse your presentation in front of an associate, friend, or spouse if possible—you may get helpful feedback, but even more important, you'll get comfortable making eye contact and using good body language. When my daughters were toddlers and I would come home late from the office needing to rehearse for a presentation the next day, I would occasionally pop one of them out of her crib, sit her on a chair, and rehearse. I remember one time one of them fell off the chair and didn't even wake up (she may have been prescient because the pitch I made the next day bombed). If all else fails, rehearse in front of a mirror.

7. Integrate any video- or audiotapes you are playing into your presentation by knowing exactly what you want to say before you play them (intro) and at their conclusion (outro). Dead silence at the end of a videotape is disconcerting. Unless there's an immediate reaction from the audience, I'll usually ask a question about the video, which frequently serves as a transition to my next point.

Learn and practice the fundamentals of rehearsing. You will not only become a better presenter, you'll win more business.

Contingency Planning

Sometimes things you can't control go amiss: Your expert cancels at the last minute with the flu. The decision maker isn't at the meeting. You failed to uncover a hidden objection. You made an erroneous assumption. Unplanned events happen to everyone. (Those who follow the Ten Rules faithfully find it happens a lot less frequently to them.) But if a "catastrophe" does arise, here's what I suggest you do:

1. Don't panic. If the exigency occurs *before* the presentation, carefully consider your options. Can you cancel the meeting without losing the sale? Can you get a replacement expert? Can you secure alternative props, samples, or the like? If you encounter a crisis *during* the presentation try asking questions either to buy time while you plan your response or to gain insight as to why you're in the pickle you now find yourself.

2. Be forthcoming. Nobody I know has ever gotten into trouble by being caught in a truth. Yes, sometimes the truth hurts, but your integrity will remain intact.

3. Don't be too hard on yourself—*unless* you didn't abide by the Ten Rules—then you have my permission to brood and sulk. Learn from your mistakes.

2.12 A FINAL THOUGHT ABOUT THE TEN RULES OF POWER PITCHING

These rules you've just read are the foundation of Power Pitching. If you truly want to give great presentations, you must at least follow the heart and soul of each rule, if not the letter.

These rules stand as a rational system for putting together and delivering very professional, very powerful business presentations. These are not binding rules that restrict behavior or expression; in fact, they do the opposite—they encourage creativity and calculated risk taking. In the remaining chapters of this book I will teach you how to shroud your presentations in powerful visuals—visuals that ring with clarity and paint stirring and memorable mind pictures.

3

Speaking the Visual Language

3.1 THE TECHNIQUES AND PRINCIPLES OF CREATING POWERFUL VISUALS

Amateurish, disjointed, simplistic, inelegant, or soiled visuals are an excellent way to communicate lack of preparation, sophistication, or commitment. I'm sure at one time or another you've seen slides or overheads or boards and said to yourself (or maybe even aloud), "what's that supposed to mean?" Have those ever been *your* slides or overheads or boards? Possibly. The goal of this chapter is to show you how to use visuals effectively to add interest, energy, and memorability to your pitch and to prevent you from ever again *knowingly* using inferior visuals that can mislead, frustrate, bore, confuse, or otherwise negatively impact you or your presentation.

I have no intention of trying to turn you into a graphic designer, videographer, cartographer, model maker, or production artist. But I do want you to be able to effectively communicate with these people—to knowledgeably direct, motivate, and judge their work. For the most part, I'll be discussing the techniques and principles associated with the presentation media you use most frequently: boards, flip charts, overheads, slides, and electronic images. Let's begin by discussing the basics of visual support design.

Design Fundamentals: The Law of Clarity, Comprehension, and Impact

The fundamentals of presentation visual design are clarity, comprehension, and impact. Each factor contributes to the creation of professional, powerful presentations. *Clarity* refers specifically to the legibility of your visuals; they absolutely must be readable. *Comprehension* addresses the issue of intelligibility; your audience must understand the message of your visual. *Impact* deals with maintaining audience interest and creating memorability by energizing your visuals—breathing life into your key points and conclusions.

I actually consider the fundamentals of presentation visual design to be laws. Urging you to obey these laws is about as close as I'll ever come to breaking the *ultimate* law of "never saying never." Allow me to explain why.

Clarity

The first law of presentation visual design is immutable—you must be certain the audience can clearly see and read the text, symbol, chart, graph, or image you're displaying. Be sensitive to backgrounds, color choices, size of text or symbols—especially charts and typefaces. 𝕮𝖆𝖓 𝖞𝖔𝖚 𝖎𝖒𝖆𝖌𝖎𝖓𝖊 𝖙𝖗𝖞𝖎𝖓𝖌 𝖙𝖔 𝖗𝖊𝖆𝖉 𝖙𝖍𝖎𝖘 𝖇𝖔𝖔𝖐 𝖎𝖓 𝖙𝖍𝖎𝖘 𝖙𝖞𝖕𝖊𝖋𝖆𝖈𝖊? or gleaning useful information from the chart in Figure 3–1?

Comprehension

The second law of presentation visual design is to be sure your audience understands the implied meaning or sense of your visual metaphors; be sure your visuals logically support your presentation remarks; be sure to organize and display data in configurations or arrangements that your audience is familiar with—and be especially wary of complex charts. Would you use the chart in Figure 3–2 to compare Acme's sales performance trend to four of its competitors? You wouldn't after reading this book.

Impact

The third law of presentation visual design is impact. Presentation impact is achieved when your visuals lend interest, strength, and memorability to your points and conclusions. Every visual doesn't have to be a Steven Spielberg production to have impact. Impact is a matter of what works best for the presentation you're making *based on the Ten Rules of Power Pitching.*

FIGURE 3–1

Unreadable Chart

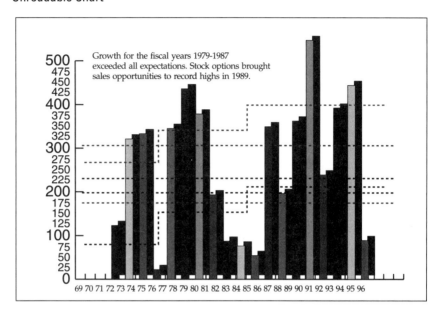

FIGURE 3–2

Unintelligible Chart

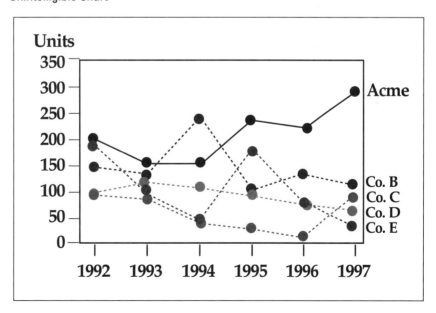

By illustration, suppose I want to make the following point: *Based on current projections, model X should be dropped from the line by the end of fiscal 1998.* Let's look at four visual approaches to support that conclusion: Figure 3–3 is distracting; the visual copy is too dissimilar from my narrative. Figure 3–4 is confusing; it fails to support my conclusion. Figure 3–5 merely parrots what I'm saying, which is helpful only to members of the audience who are deaf. Figure 3–6 supports and enhances my point in a traditional fashion. Figure 3–7 also supports and enhances my point, but in a lighthearted manner. In the latter two cases, the tone of your presentation and the character of the audience would determine which visual would have the greatest impact.

Figure 3–8 contains examples of visual impact vis-à-vis common presentation claims or conclusions. These are the types of visuals you want to use to support *your* presentation.

Design fundamentals should be looked upon as the "grammar rules" of the language of visual communications. To achieve success at any endeavor—be it music, dance, woodworking, art, or sports—one must first learn and practice the fundamentals.

FIGURE 3–3

Impact Illustration Visual #1

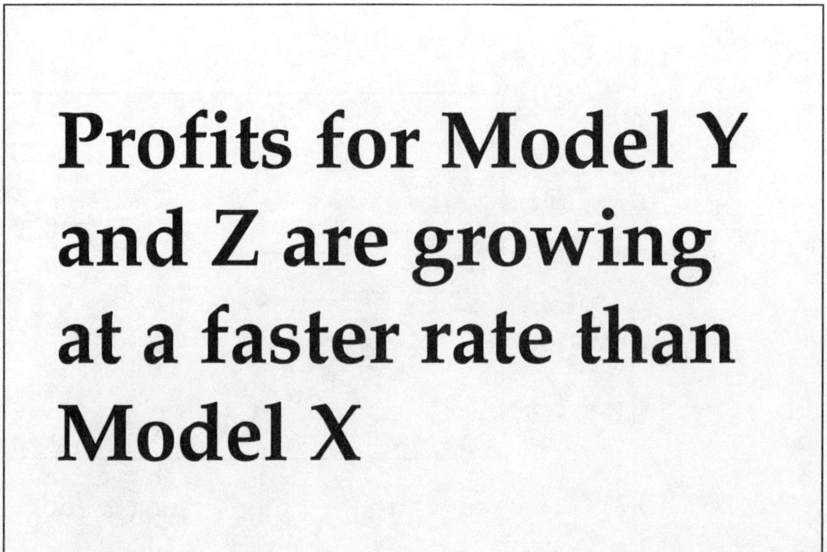

Profits for Model Y and Z are growing at a faster rate than Model X

FIGURE 3–4

Impact Illustration Visual #2

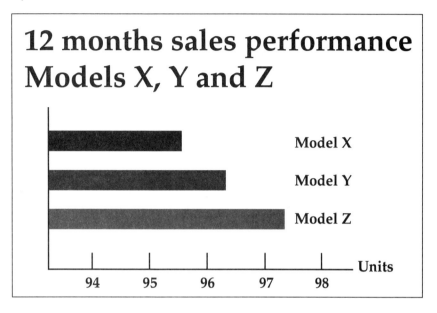

FIGURE 3–5

Impact Illustration Visual #3

Based on current projections, Model X should be dropped from the line by the end of fiscal 1998

Impact Illustration Visual #4

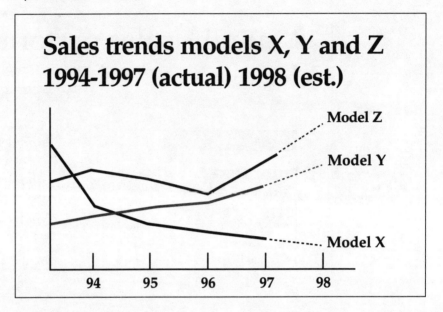

Sales trends models X, Y and Z 1994-1997 (actual) 1998 (est.)

Impact Illustration Visual #5

FIGURE 3–8

Visual Impact

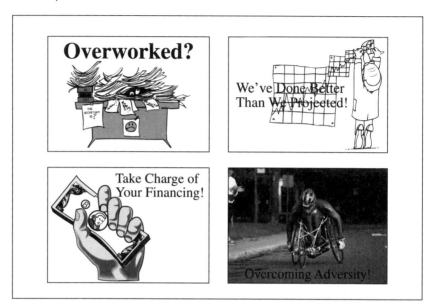

Now before you go forward, I suggest you go back and again read this brief section on design fundamentals. I want you to have the concepts of clarity, comprehension, and impact firmly seated before studying the elements of the visual language.

3.2 USING THE LANGUAGE OF VISUAL COMMUNICATIONS: TEXT, SYMBOLS, CHARTS AND GRAPHS, AND IMAGERY

Earlier, I introduced you to the language of visual communications and told you that understanding and effectively employing the visual language allows you to communicate with greater precision and impact. Now let me show you how to use this language by examining its components in greater detail, and in the context of the design fundamentals we just reviewed. Rest assured, it's not a difficult language to learn and master.

Text

Text refers to words or copy that help inform, embellish, clarify, support or distinguish a point or conclusion.

Text is the most literal dimension of the visual language (like nouns that specifically refer to persons, places, things, states, or qualities). As such, special care must be taken with respect to the selection and display of text.

1. Use terminology your audience will understand.

Don't use industry jargon (especially your own industry's) unless you are absolutely certain your audience understands the meaning of those terms. On the other hand, using industry terminology familiar to your customer or prospect can *positively* impact your presentation.

2. Avoid five-dollar words like the plague.

Sales presentations are not the time or place to show off your vocabulary, save it for the Sunday *New York Times* crossword puzzle. There's an old maxim I have always followed when it comes to presentation audiences: Never *underestimate* their intelligence and never *overestimate* their knowledge. I urge you to follow this principle relentlessly.

3. Be consistent in your use of terminology.

As I discussed earlier, you must use virtually the same words or phrases that appear on your visuals when you speak. Don't run the risk of confusing or distracting your audience.

4. Use action or hot-button words or phrases to support your presentation. These words or phrases will strengthen the point or conclusion you're making, add character to your presentation, and increase memorability. These terms may be industry specific (to your customer or prospect of course) or terms familiar to the populace at large (e.g., powerhouse, lightning rod, surging, Internet, synergy, download, networking, empower).

5. Use legible typefaces and backgrounds.

I can't stress this point often enough—be sure the text is easy to read. Use crisp, clean type (hand-lettered boards must be neatly printed) against backgrounds that *encourage* rather than *discourage* readership. If I seem to be obsessive about this point it's because I've seen so much abuse of this basic tenet of visual communications over the years—even by professionals. My favorite (but sad) story that illustrates such abuse was committed by a trade magazine publisher acquaintance of mine who was launching a new publication. I happened to be in his office shortly after the inaugural issue was printed, and I knew he was eager to show it to me. As I flipped through it, I was stopped cold by his "Letter from the Publisher" column. It was absolutely illegible. He had used a rather delicate serif typeface printed over a medium green background that was peppered with light dashes (a short-lived early 1990s graphic design fad). I was speechless. I just didn't have the heart to rip him. Two years later his business went BK.

(Okay, so my editor says, "What's BK?" I tell him, "BK is lawyer jargon for bankrupt." "Look," he says, "you can't use the term *BK;* your readers may not understand what it means; they can't even look it up in a dictionary; it's annoying." Say, where have you heard that before?)

6. Be a copy minimalist.

Legible typefaces against proper backgrounds are of little consequence if you attempt to put "The Collected Speeches of Winston Churchill" on a couple of slides. Too much copy is distracting and generally causes the visual to be unreadable—even when projected on a screen through an overhead projector, slide projector, or LCD projector. As I've mentioned before, limit the text to the essence of the point or conclusion you're making. If necessary, break a wordy visual into two or three parts. No points are deducted for extra visuals, but just one unreadable visual could ruin your day.

7. Use typefaces to add interest or character.

You can increase audience attentiveness and memorability through the judicious selection and application of typefaces:

A WESTERN MOTIF

The Elegance of Art Deco

INDUSTRIAL STRENGTH

JOURNEY TO THE MIDDLE EAST

A Delicate Touch

Stroll Down Park Avenue

Be careful not to overuse this device. It should be used like a fine chef uses herbs and spices—just enough to add a dash of distinction.

Symbols

Symbols are visual impressions of known signs or representations that create impact, interest or add memorability.

Symbols are the interjections and idioms of the visual language. In office buildings, on highways, on packaging, in retail stores, in your automobile—just about anywhere you go you see symbols that quickly and efficiently instruct, direct, inform, and alert. What a huge vocabulary we have at our disposal!

F I G U R E   3–9

Symbols as Shorthand

1. Use symbols as shorthand to underscore points and conclusions. The symbols represented in Figure 3–9 need no explanation.

2. Use symbols as transitions.

Symbols are a wonderful device for transitioning from one section or aspect of your presentation to another. They add continuity and interest. Symbols are extremely helpful in creating presentation themes. (I'll talk more about themes in Chapter 5).

3. Symbols can add interest to or lighten up a presentation.

For example, fruits and vegetables can be powerful, memorable symbols. Just about everyone knows the symbology of apples, lemons, plums, pickles, (sour) grapes, peas (in a pod), carrots (on a stick), and the ever popular banana (peel). Animals too—from the king of the jungle to a barrel full of monkeys to the odoriferous skunk. You can talk about a *problem* and visually display a dark cloud; when you talk about your *solution* bring out a bright sun. You can illustrate time using the sun (rising and setting); the moon (growing from a sliver to full); or an acorn (becoming an oak). Flags, signs of the zodiac, playing cards, computer icons, road signs, the top of a keyboard—!@#$%^&*()_+—I can give you pages and pages of examples. But I'll spare you. I think you've got the 💡.

Charts and Graphs

Charts and graphs organize information in various formats (tables, maps, lines, bars, curves), representing historic or projected data, functions, or relationships.

Recognizing that entire books have been written on this subject, I will limit my discussion to business-presentation chart and graph fundamentals and strategies. Incidentally, purists would not necessarily lump charts and graphs together; technically, they are distinct. However, I believe the net effect of charts and graphs (simplification and clarification) merits their coalescence when talking about the language of visual communications. To keep our simile alive, we can compare charts and graphs to pronouns, which replace nouns and noun clauses. Regardless of how charts are designed, decorated, or configured, there are only four basic formats: pie charts, bar charts (horizontal or vertical), line charts, and dot charts (also called scatter diagrams). Figure 3–10 represents these basic chart formats.

Knowing how and when to use charts and graphs is integral to the effective use of the language of visual communications. It's like knowing the alphabet—how could you spell or read without knowing your ABCs?

FIGURE 3–10

The Four Basic Chart Formats

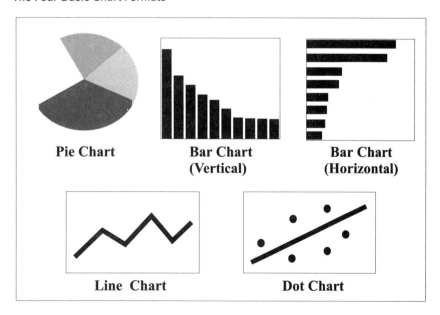

Pie Chart	Bar Chart (Vertical)	Bar Chart (Horizontal)
Line Chart	Dot Chart	

The alphabet of the language of visual communications begins with the letters *QC*.

Introducing the QC Factor

Be sure the chart or graph you're using can *quickly* and *clearly* make your point.

The QC factor is a corollary to the design fundamentals of clarity, comprehension, and impact. Selecting the proper chart is a matter of first determining what you want to say (communications objective) and then selecting the chart format that best achieves that objective. If the chart you've produced doesn't immediately and unambiguously make your point, nuke it. Try another format or consider another approach (possibly a table or a series of charts). Let's look at a few examples of good charts and bad charts.

CASE 1

COMPARISON OF MARKET SHARE
Acme versus Leading Competitors

The line chart in Figure 3–11 (left) makes no sense here; it fails the QC test. (To someone not paying close attention to what the speaker is saying, this

FIGURE 3–11

Case One—Line Chart versus Bar Chart

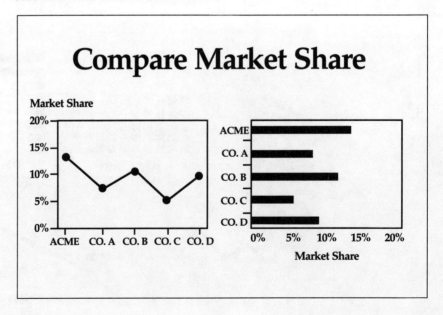

chart would imply that Acme's market share is unstable.) The bar chart in Figure 3–11 (right) not only quickly and clearly says Acme's market share is highest among its competitors but also places Acme at the *top of the list*—one of those positive connotations that supports my contention that if you have command of the visual language you can create more powerful presentations.

CASE 2

ACME'S SALES TREND
1992–1997

By our QC standards, the bar chart in Figure 3–12 (left) is the wrong choice—once again the viewer not paying close attention could be misled (are sales trending down?). The line chart in Figure 3–12 (right) makes obvious sense because even casual viewers understand the implications of an upward sloping line or curve.

As an aside, there are times when designers consciously make the "wrong choice." When public companies have one or two bad years following a series of up years, they will often tip their bar charts over to ease the negative visual impact (Figure 3–13). Keep that in mind the next time you're looking through an annual report and you come across horizontal bar charts—chances are the letter to shareholders will start out: "Last year was a challenging time for . . ." Check it out.

FIGURE 3–12

Case Two—Bar Chart versus Line Chart

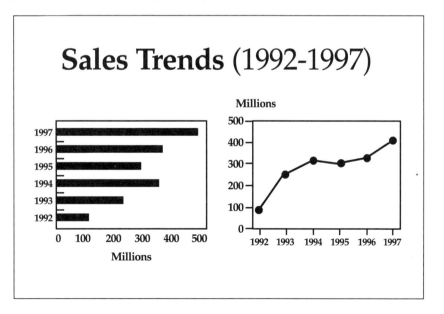

FIGURE 3–13

Tipping Over the Bar Charts

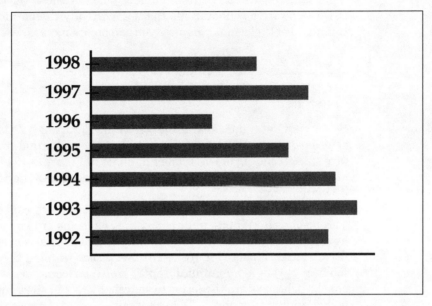

CASE 3

COMPARISON OF SALES TRENDS
Acme versus Leading Competitors (1992–1997)

The dot chart in Figure 3–14 (left) in this case is one of those "what the hell is that supposed to mean?" visuals. The double vertical bar chart in Figure 3–14 (right) is totally "QC."

CASE 4

ACME'S PERFORMANCE
Compared to Four of Its Competitors

You probably thought I forgot about this "hair weave" chart (Figure 3–15) I used earlier as an example of poor visual communications. Not so. The solution (as always) begins with the communications objective—we want to compare Acme's performance to the performance of four other companies. Let's say that it *isn't* necessary to include all performance trends on one chart. A series of charts will then neatly serve our purpose (Figure 3–16). Key points can be made quickly and clearly by spending a little time on each comparison, instead of asking the audience to read between, through, over, and

FIGURE 3–14

Case Three—Dot Chart versus Bar Chart

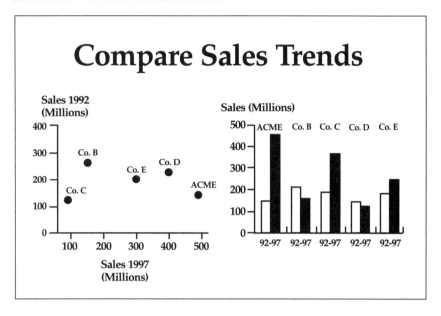

FIGURE 3–15

Unintelligible Chart

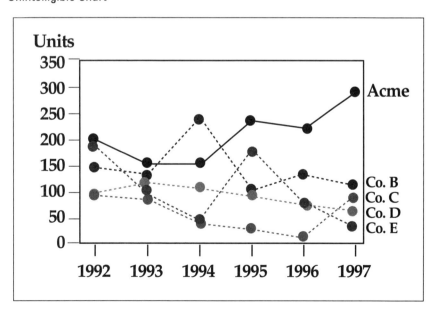

FIGURE 3–16

Case Four—Four Line Charts

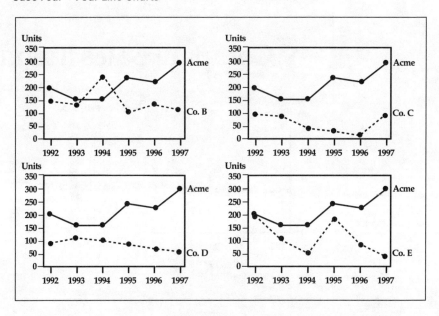

under the lines. I might argue the comparison is even more powerful because of the *aggregate* impression being made (four times more powerful?).

But what if it *is* necessary to include all performance trends on one chart or graph? Then a table would probably be the best choice for allowing data to be compared over a specific time frame (Figure 3–17). Wouldn't you agree this is more effective and more meaningful than the original line chart?

CASE 5

COMPANY A's 15 DISTRIBUTION CENTERS
Located Strategically Throughout the United States

Here's another an example of failing to meet the communications objective, the pie chart on the left in Figure 3–18 doesn't adequately support the strategic location claim. Visual power is created by using the map on the right in Figure 3–18 to pinpoint distribution center locations. The map also provides the means to highlight any location that may be especially significant to your audience.

I want you to realize that the use of ill-conceived charts is not as extreme or rare an occurrence as you may believe. Over the years I have seen charts and graphs just as fatuous as the ones we've just

FIGURE 3–17

Condensing Chart Data Into a Table

Sales Performance 1992-1997
Acme vs. Leading Competitors

	% Increase (Decrease) 1992-1997
Acme	50%
Company B	(15)
Company C	0
Company D	(25)
Company E	(75)

FIGURE 3–18

Case Five—Pie Chart and Map

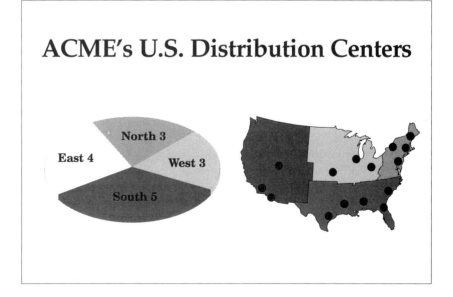

ACME's U.S. Distribution Centers

East 4 / North 3 / West 3 / South 5

reviewed. The lesson to be learned is that you *must* take the time to review and challenge each chart and graph you plan to use in your presentation: Does it achieve the communications objective? Does it pass the QC test? If you're uncertain, ask your associates if they understand the point you are trying to make. If they don't, you can remedy the problem and be thankful you were smart enough to make the change before you prejudiced yourself in front of your audience.

Charts with an Attitude

Create charts and graphs that complement the tone of your presentation. By adding a little character to your charts and graphs, you can measurably increase presentation interest and memorability. Moreover, the "customized" look of your presentation helps you tell clients or prospects they're special. First consider the tone of your presentation. Is it serious, light, technical, fast paced, or whimsical? Your charts and graphs can help reflect that tone. Let's suppose I'm pitching a pickle company. I might create some visuals using "Picklese" (See Figure 3–19 on page I–1 of the color insert) one of the many dialects of the language of visual communications.

Your opportunities to add character to your presentation are limitless as you can see in the examples represented in Figure 3–20 on page I–2 of the color insert.

Presentation Stress

Utilize graphic elements to help call out your points and conclusions. You can use colors; typefaces; and type weight or size to highlight key data on your visuals. Sexier options are available when creating electronic images, slides, or overheads. The tone of your presentation will guide your choice of options. Figure 3–21 illustrates common examples of highlighting.

Some Final Thoughts on Charts and Graphs

As I mentioned earlier, it's likely that you'll be working with a creative resource who will be responsible for producing the presentation visuals. Visual production can be a real crapshoot (pun intended). Some resources are very talented and will be able to help you design brilliant charts and dazzling graphs. Many are not so talented and will only be able to give you what you give them. Only neater. In any case, the ultimate QC responsibility rests squarely on your shoulders. Consequently, if you feel you need a good basic (and beyond) lesson in

FIGURE 3–19

The Pickle Examples

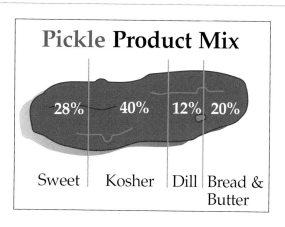

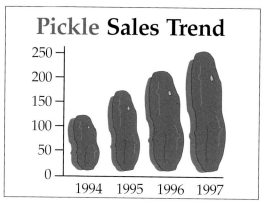

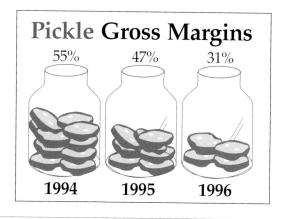

FIGURE 3–20

Adding Character to Your Presentation

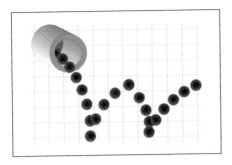

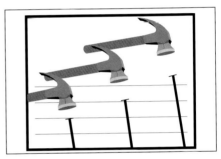

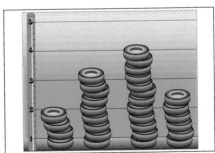

FIGURE 3–23

White on Black versus Black on White

Based on current projections, Model X should be dropped from the line by the end of fiscal 1998

Based on current projections, Model X should be dropped from the line by the end of fiscal 1998

FIGURE 4–2A

Competition's Slide Presentation—Acme Fruit Juice Co.

F I G U R E 4–2B

Competition's Slide Presentation—Acme Fruit Juice Co.

Packaging
Expertise
from Soup
to Nuts

- Sauces
- Vegetables
- Baked goods
- Beverages
- Frozen Foods
- Condiments
- Lots More

ALL MATERIALS
° Glass
  ° Metal
    ° Plastic

A Leader
in
Packaging
*For Over
30
Years!*

Special Packaging?

No Problem!

F I G U R E 4–3

Presentation Titles with Situation Overviews

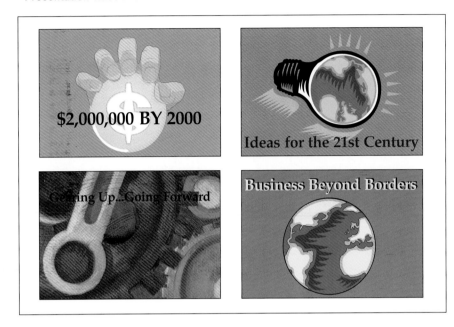

F I G U R E 4–7

Four Disparate Photo Images

FIGURE 4–8

Four Images in Grid

FIGURE 4–9

Same Photo—Four Versions

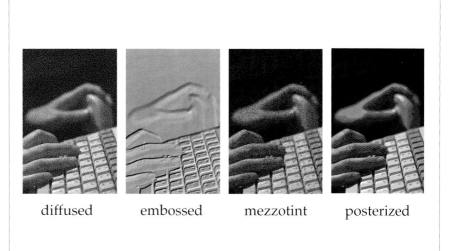

FIGURE 5–1

Spending Time with One Chart—"Get Creative"

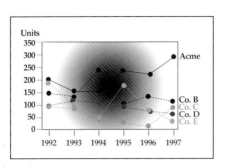

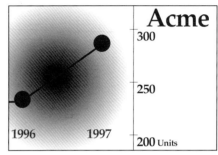

FIGURE 3–21

Highlighting

Based on current projections, **Model X** should be dropped from the line by the end of *fiscal 1998*

Based on **CURRENT** projections, Model X should be <u>dropped</u> from the line by the end of fiscal 1998

Based on current **PROJECTIONS**, Model X should be dropped from the line by the *end of fiscal* 1998

charts and graphs, I suggest you pick up a copy of *Say It with Charts* by Gene Zelazny (Irwin), an easy-reading, informative book that will truly enlighten you.

I am also well aware of the fact that there is quite a bit of software around today—PowerPoint, Freelance, Astound, for example—that has turned many a salesperson into a part-time graphic designer/production artist with singular responsibility for presentation content. If that's you, I implore you to not get caught up in the gimmicks of this software. Concentrate on substance. As I stated very early on, *you* are the focal point of the sales presentation; visuals are your tools. I'll have more to say about electronic imaging and its impact on salespeople later on. I'd wager you already have a pretty good idea where I stand on this particular factoid of life.

Imagery

Images are photographs or graphic representations (illustrations) that create settings, moods or trigger emotions.

Images are the adjectives and adverbs of the visual language. They expand upon ideas, crystalize, inspire, excite, and stimulate.

Images are the most potent component of the visual language because of their range: from literal to abstract; from analytical to fanciful; from benign to emotionally charged. The power is in the execution, which spans a continuum ranging from realism to impressionism. For example, a photograph of a Jaguar XJS in a dealer's showroom makes one statement; a photograph of the same car pulling into a luxury hotel with an admiring doorman saluting the driver makes another; and a long shot of the Jag on a lonesome desert road at sunset makes still another. Compare a realistic illustration of a Jaguar to a concept drawing of the car. Are they making the same statement? Of course not.

As we continue our discussion of images please note that when I refer to "photography," I am also including videography and cinematography (where applicable), and when I refer to illustrations, I'm also talking about animation (where applicable). Also, while not denying the existence of photo impressionism or artistic realism, we shall agree the principal difference between photography and illustration is that photography provides literal reproductions of subject matter, while illustrations are interpretive (conceptual).

1. *Do not use images that are amateurish or of inferior quality.* "Art" is subjective, who's to say what's good photography or illustration and what isn't? Especially when you consider the rampant and often passionate disagreements among respected movie, book, music, and art critics. To be certain, artistic quality is a gray area. But we're not talking about fine art here; we're talking about business-presentation art, which has a specific purpose. And your critics—your fellow employees, distributors, vendors, financial analysts, customers, and prospects—are far more consequential than those imperious dilettantes, Siskel and Ebert. It should come as no surprise to you that I believe cheesy, cheap images can make you or your organization look cheesy and cheap. I also believe it's possible to take much of the subjectivity out of the evaluation equation. Here's how:

- Be sure all illustrations and photographs meet the criteria of design fundamentals and pass the QC test.

- Be sure the image satisfies your communications objective.

- Examine your images from the audience's point of view. Be sure they reflect well on you and your organization. Ask yourself, What would I think of the person or company displaying these images? If you can't respond positively, or are in doubt, take action to correct the problem or get another opinion or two from people you respect.

♦ Don't settle for "it's good enough." Good enough isn't even average.

This last point reminds me of a client I had many years ago who was awarded an Olympic Gold Medal for not having a clue. The client was the director of communications of a Fortune 500 company. We were helping his staff put together an internal communications program designed to inspire and motivate the corporation's 25,000-plus employees. He had themed his program "Beyond the Minimal." Susan Mahoney, our sales director (intuitive, tenacious, motivated—one of the best salespeople I have ever known), was handling the account. She came to me one day and said that the client was unhappy with the production aspects of the project, in particular the typesetting, and would I meet with him. Naturally, I said yes. I then took my first critical look at the project and immediately called Susan into my office. I could barely contain myself, "Why is he calling this program 'Beyond the Minimal'? Doesn't anyone over there realize that *minimal* is like a D-minus; a D could be beyond the minimal!—I mean, beyond the minimal isn't even average—a C is average?! and what's wrong with the typesetting?"

Susan mentioned that a few of his staffers were bemused by the title but were reluctant to confront him, and she didn't know what was wrong with the typesetting. Finally, I told Susan we should raise our doubts about the program's theme to him; it was our duty as professionals. Susan was tentative, but by now I was driven to enlighten this man. We had our meeting a few days later at his office. I told him I was eager to address and help solve his production concerns, but I first wanted to mention our apprehension about the program's theme. He listened icily to my perspicacious rationale and dismissed it out of hand. He then pulled out a loupe (a magnifying glass used by printers) to show me how the kerning (the space between letters) was improperly executed. "Sloppy," I believe was his exact word. Walking back to our office I turned to Susan and said, "Can you believe it, he was all worked up over an imaginary typesetting problem, but couldn't appreciate the fact that his program theme could be easily misinterpreted or even ridiculed." She nodded a sad assent.

Well, I certainly hope *you* don't know people who are that vain and shortsighted. But if you do, perhaps you can convince them to open their minds and let their brains grow bigger than their egos.

2. *Use photography to document/support a point or conclusion.* Photography is an excellent way to dispel audience skepticism. It's hard to argue with photographic proof of claims.

3. *Use illustrations to represent concepts.* A proposed office building, a new line of jogging suits, an ad campaign, a redesigned machine tool, a floor plan, how an antidepressant works in the brain, a reorganization—no argument about it, *good* illustrations will help you position and sell your ideas more effectively. As we just discussed, style matters. Look professional. Make sure the execution of your illustrations enhances your ideas: A machine tool should have a feeling of "precision"; a line of jogging suits should look "fashionable"; the pharmacodynamics of a drug should emanate an aura of "science." Don't settle for anything less.

4. *Photography gives you the means to offer facility tours in the comfort of an office, conference room, or auditorium.* Assume you're a salesperson and your customer or prospect does not have the time or means to inspect your operations but wants to be assured you have the capacity and resources to meet its requirements. You could talk, talk, talk, all day long, but no amount of conversation could possibly be as effective as a five-minute photographic tour of your company to remove any trace of uncertainty as to your capabilities. It's the only way to fly.

5. *You can create powerful testimonials using videography.* Letters of praise are nice, but videos are absolutely the best way to introduce your audience to people who are glad they use your products or services or have "signed on" to your program. Testimonials add tremendous credibility and energy to your presentation. Not only does your audience empathize with the people offering testimonials; they recognize that those people are not being paid a salary or commission to say all those nice things about you. In fact, I personally consider a well-produced testimonial-documentary style video to be the "mother of all sales tools"; it's the most powerful selling tool any business can provide to its sales force.

6. *Photography or illustration can add humor to your presentation.* As I said earlier in this book (Rule Eight), humor can be problematic to sales presentations. Jokes can bomb or offend more often than you might imagine; that's why I prefer clever, purposeful stories or anecdotes (with the caution that you must be careful not to insult anybody or make yourself look foolish). Here are my views on the subject of using images to add humor to business presentations.

♦ Think twice about using the funny papers.

Personally, I don't particularly care for cartoons that have been appropriated from print media, even if there is a point to their being included. Frankly, I'd rather create my own cartoons. I can have them customized or personalized as appropriate. But please, be sure you have your ideas implemented by a good cartoonist. If one isn't available, I strongly urge you to come up with another idea (yes, there's always "Dilbert").

◆ Humorous images can add emphasis and increase memorability.

I pointed this out earlier when we discussed symbols and their ability to lighten up a presentation. Photography or illustration is your means for executing this tactic.

◆ Do not use socially unacceptable images.

I follow this rule: If it won't play at a PTA luncheon, it shouldn't play at a business meeting.

◆ Don't make fun of your competitors.

Unflattering cartoons or illustrations slamming your competition may be more harmful than helpful to your cause.

7. *Use photographs or illustrations to help create presentation continuity.* The use of good *quality* images to create continuity and give your presentation a professional finish is sorely underutilized. (As I'm sure you've noticed, I'm uncompromising about image quality; I hope I can convince you to be just as stubborn.) A recurring theme illustration, a series of related photographs, a format incorporating photos or illustrations are all viable continuity techniques. I'll be talking more about continuity as a *presentation* fundamental in the next section of this book.

8. *Photography can reduce to human scale or blow up to epic scale.* The magic of photography is its uncanny ability to so deeply move its viewers. Imagine you want to convince a customer or prospect that your company is not cold, gray, and impersonal but in fact is vital, vibrant, and brimming with people who take pride in their work, pride in their company, and genuinely care about satisfying their customers. Short of having that customer or prospect meet those people first hand, the most compelling way you can tell that story is through a well-produced photo essay or a video showing people (not machines) performing their tasks with care, concern, and enthusiasm.

Or suppose you are a small company that wants to look big and imposing. Photography can create that illusion. Back in the days when diversified conglomerates were the rage, Swift-Eckrich (a Beatrice company) hired us to produce a video about precooked bacon and bacon bits for its foodservice group. We taped the video in Omaha,

Nebraska. The precooked bacon operations area (from cooking to packing) was the size of a racquetball court. The "cooking" was done in a big microwave oven that was managed by three people; bacon bits were cooked in a pipe that ran around the ceiling. The packaging for both products was done by hand: the precooked bacon in boxes; the bacon bits in big foodservice-sized cans. The product managers told us they wanted the video to make their operation look "high tech." We accomplished our task by using a lot of extreme close-ups of the product and equipment and eliminated people from all cooking or packing shots (e.g., we'd show a close-up of the can's lid being sealed without revealing the guy standing beside it turning a crank). In the final edit we used a lot of cutaways—exteriors of the plant, livestock, slaughter houses, dials, gauges, forklifts, loading docks, foodservice applications, and so on. The finished product was a hit. Our client was as happy as a pig in a puddle. Such is the magic of videography. (You didn't really think Forrest Gump shook hands with JFK, did you?)

3.3 COLOR YOUR REMARKS

Color is a great deal more than visual decoration. Visual clarity, comprehension and impact can be strongly influenced by color choices. I want you to be aware of how color choices affect legibility, interest, and memorability.

1. *Select your background colors carefully.*

Slides and overheads virtually always look better when sporting dark backgrounds. Because slides and overheads are produced on film or acetate and projected (magnified) on a screen or bright surface, dirt is an issue. Light backgrounds readily expose dust or dirt on the film as well as any discolorations or smudges that may be on the screen or wall upon which you're projecting. Luckily, dark backgrounds obfuscate dirt. On the other hand, print media is easier to read (remember clarity!) against a white or light background. Compare the following: I'm sure you'll agree the copy that's reversed in Figure 3–22 is more difficult to read than the copy printed black on white. (See, also, Figure 3–23 on page I–3 of the color insert.) I call this "visual noise." Incidentally, you would never want to create a slide with this much copy on it. An overhead could handle this much copy (and frequently does for internal meetings) but not for most business presentations—especially sales presentations.

2. *Colors can help you underscore key points.*

Changing the color of a headline, a subhead, or a word or number in a sentence or a list of words or numbers is the equivalent of

FIGURE 3–22

White on Black versus Black on White

Four score and seven years ago our fathers brought forth onto this continent a new nation, conceived in liberty and dedicated to the proposition that all men are created equal. Now we are engaged in a great Civil War, testing whether this nation, or any nation so conceived, and so dedicated, can long endure, we are met on a great battlefield of that war. We have come to dedicate a portion of that field, as a final resting place for those here who gave their lives that this nation might live.

Four score and seven years ago our fathers brought forth onto this continent a new nation, conceived in liberty and dedicated to the proposition that all men are created equal. Now we are engaged in a great Civil War, testing whether this nation, or any nation so conceived, and so dedicated, can long endure, we are met on a great battlefield of that war. We have come to dedicate a portion of that field, as a final resting place for those here who gave their lives that this nation might live.

underlining, **boldfacing,** or *italicizing*—in fact, color is often the most effective way to call attention to the key point or conclusion of your visual.

3. *Colors can help you create moods, build motifs, or stir emotions.*

Certain colors or color combinations complement concepts or evoke mental images. For example:

Red = Hot/Exciting

Gray = Conservative/Calculated

Gold = Success/Opportunity

Black = Threatening/Doom

Green = Money/Grass

Blue = Sky/Water/Clarity

Yellow = Telegram/Taxi

Red and Green = Christmas

Green and Yellow = Springtime

Red, White, and Blue = USA (or France or England)

F I G U R E 3–24A

One Visual per Feature

F I G U R E 3–24B

One Visual Noting All Features

ZAPGUARD

° **Durable**

ZAPGUARD

° **Durable**
° **Easily Upgraded**
° **Simple to Operate**
° **Reliable**

ZAPGUARD

° **Easily Upgraded**

ZAPGUARD

° **Simple to Update**

ZAPGUARD

° **Reliable**

FIGURE 3–25

The Build and Subdue Method

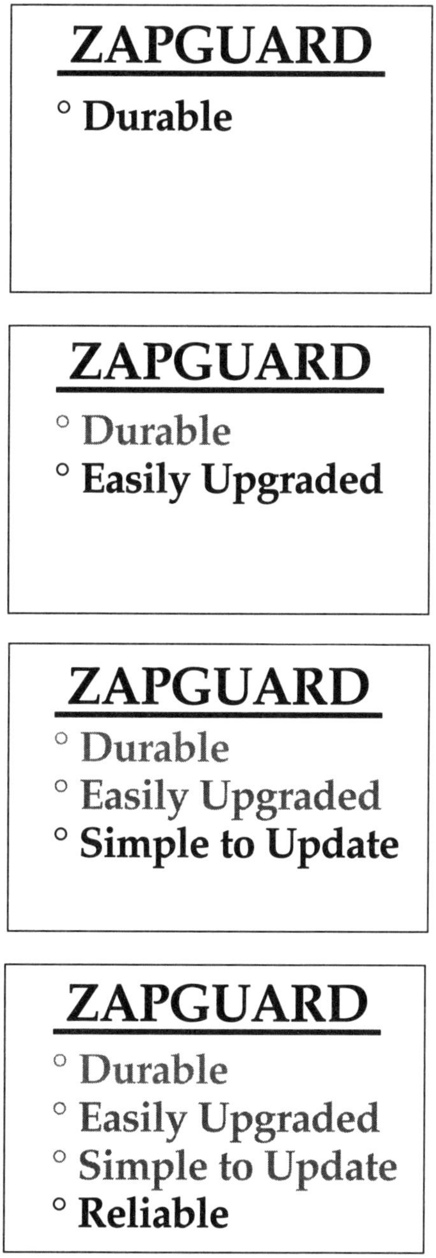

ZAPGUARD
° **Durable**

ZAPGUARD
° Durable
° **Easily Upgraded**

ZAPGUARD
° Durable
° Easily Upgraded
° **Simple to Update**

ZAPGUARD
° Durable
° Easily Upgraded
° Simple to Update
° **Reliable**

Country colors, college colors, corporate colors, or brand colors may also be just what you need to add interest and spark to your presentation. Under certain circumstances I would even consider plaids and stripes to be colors. Try to use these special colors in a fresh, tasteful way. Your customer or prospect will likely be impressed with your creativity.

4. *Colors can help you lead your audience through a presentation topic.*

A technique called "build and subdue" can help you discuss topics/subtopics in an orderly and memorable fashion. Let's assume you want to discuss the features of an Acme ZapGuard. A ZapGuard is durable; it can be easily upgraded; it's simple to operate and very reliable. The traditional options are to (1) create four visuals—one for each feature (Figure 3–24A) or (2) create one visual noting all four features (Figure 3–24B)

The *build-and-subdue* method is sort of the best of both worlds. It works like this:

As Figure 3–25 illustrates, as you discuss the virtues of the ZapGuard, the particular feature you're discussing is highlighted (e.g., using white or a bright color against a dark background) while features you've already discussed are subdued (by toning down the text). Your visuals *literally* support the build up of your features story. Hence the designation, build and subdue.

Walking the Walk

You have now been exposed to the Ten Rules of Power Pitching. You are familiar with the fundamentals of presentation visual support design, the language of visual communications, and the role color plays in creating powerful visuals. You can now talk the talk. In the next section I'll introduce you to the fundamentals of presentation design—the final step to proficiency in power pitching.

4

Power Pitching

The Principles of Visual Presentation Design

In Chapter 3, our discussion of the fundamentals of presentation visual design and the language of visual communications was limited to the *singular* creation of powerful visuals. In this Chapter, you'll learn the most effective way to dynamically bring these powerful visuals together.

4.1 SHARPENING YOUR TOOLS

The Ten Rules of Power Pitching. The fundamentals of visual design. The language of visual communications. These are the tools to create powerful presentations.

The political conventions of 1996 were power presentation clinics. The use of images, symbols, text, music, and staging effects was brilliant. I have rarely seen videowalls used with such skill. Even when viewed at home, on ordinary color television sets, the power of these presentations was profound. I recall seeing an ABC "Nightline" program a few days after the Democratic convention where a panel of "undecideds," who had watched both conventions on their TVs, were asked if they were influenced by either of the conventions. I was not surprised to hear the majority confess to being moved or swayed by one or more of these power presentations. The finale of the Democratic convention (President Clinton's acceptance speech) was spectacular. The sparkling confetti, the balloons, the lights, the music, the energy—it was inspired. (Let's give credit to the producers of that finale for understanding and taking advantage of the Chicago United Center's unique design characteristics to enhance that presentation.)

There's no question that you can motivate audiences with powerful presentations. How *effectively* you motivate them is a matter of how well you use your tools. Be sure those tools are sharp.

Primary and Supporting Presentation Media

Let's begin by talking about presentation media. To this point, I've discussed presentation media in general terms (in relation to planning and organization, visual design fundamentals, and the language of visual communications). Now it's necessary to look at these media specifically as they relate to sales presentations. Presentation media fall into two categories: *primary* and *supporting*.

Primary Presentation Media

Primary presentation media carry data, symbols, or images that facilitate the presentation process (i.e., "live" interactive business presentations) and, by themselves, can sustain a complete presentation. There are five primary business presentation media:

- ◆ Boards.
- ◆ Formal (written) proposals.
- ◆ Overhead transparencies.
- ◆ 35mm slides.
- ◆ Electronic images (generated on a PC screen or projected on a reflective surface).

These are the media most commonly used to deliver business presentations. In Chapter 5 I'll talk about primary presentation media at length. I believe you'll be enlightened, entertained and, in a few instances, even surprised by what I have to say.

Supporting Presentation Media

Presentation media that do not meet the criteria to be categorized as "primary" are regarded as supporting presentation media. Business presentations often incorporate prototypes, brochures, product samples, reprints of articles, and the like to add depth, impact, and memorability. The most prominent member of the supporting presentation media family is video. Chapter 6 of this book is devoted entirely to this fascinating and unbelievably powerful presentation tool.

4.2 VIP: VISUAL IMPRESSION PRINCIPLE

Think about this. You pick up an unfamiliar magazine, quickly thumb through its pages and then put it down. Without having read a single word, you've formulated an opinion about the character and quality of that publication. How? By its *visual impression:* the caliber and styling of the typography, layout, illustrations, and photography; the virtues of the paper and printing. If your visual impression is *positive,* you will tend to want read the magazine and (at least initially) be open-minded to its reportage and opinions. If your visual impression is *negative,* your interest in reading the magazine will be low; and if you do read it, you're certain to be somewhat skeptical of its content. It's only human nature. Understanding and addressing this principle is fundamental to creating powerful sales presentations. Allow me to use a visual (see Figure 4–1) to burn this VIP—very important principle—into your memory.

How does this principle bias business presentations? Well, clearly, what you don't want to do is create negative impressions. You

FIGURE 4-1

Visual Impression Principle

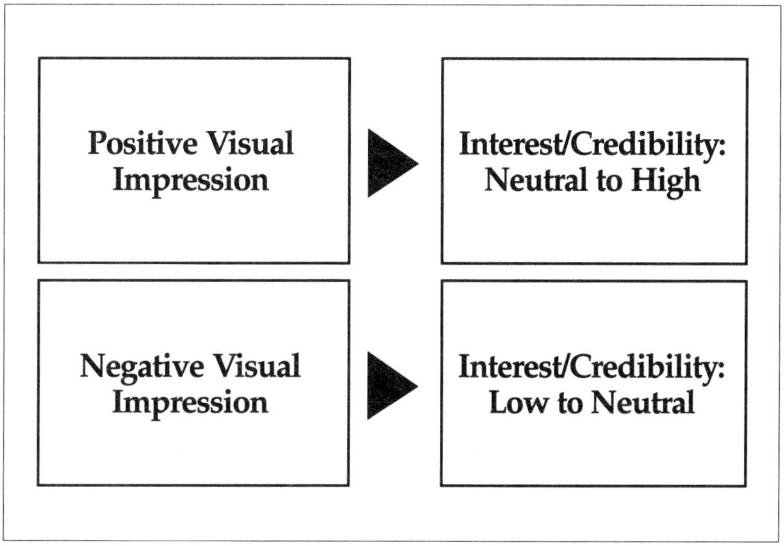

don't want your presentation to look like it was thrown together at the last second using warmed-over visuals loosely assembled from presentations past. A presentation of that sort tells your audience they don't merit special attention or consideration—a statement guaranteed to dampen their interest and weaken your credibility. What you *do* want to do is create positive impressions. You want to tell your audiences that indeed they merit a presentation put together especially for them. That sort of statement piques audience interest and builds respect.

In part, creating positive impressions is accomplished by maintaining an aesthetic consistency to the look and style of your visuals. To illustrate, let's examine a section from two slide presentations prepared by two competitors pitching the Acme Fruit Juice Co.

Figure 4–2A (on page I-4 of the color insert) represents a presentation that gives every appearance of being customized for the Acme Fruit Juice Co. The slides have a conforming look and style. Acme's name has been incorporated into the presentation. There are even little fruit images. The visual impression is positive. And there's a bonus. Beyond telling customers or prospects their business is important to you, visual continuity speaks well of you: It says you're organized, professional, committed, sincere, creative, and lots of other good things that positively impact you and the image of your company.

Figure 4–2B (on page I-5 of the color insert) represents a presentation that has been picked up from existing slides. As you can readily see, the formats are inconsistent, the text is in general terms, and there is no direct reference to Acme or its products. The visual impression is negative.

So which set of slides would you want to use if you were going to pitch for Acme's business? Me too (unless my father-in-law was the chairman of the board of the Acme Fruit Juice Co).

You might think that I exaggerated the comparison of these presentations to make my point. But you'd be wrong. I can assure you I've seen worse; my guess is, you probably have too. Let's use the visual impression principle as a springboard into our discussion of visual presentation design and organization.

4.3 THEMES ARE NOT JUST FOR PARKS

I like themes. In fact, the best way I know of to begin producing a presentation is to develop a theme—it helps me focus my thinking. Most dictionaries define *theme* as a "unifying idea or motif." Borrowing from that definition, I would define *business presentation theme* as a "unifying look and point of view." For clarification, let's break that down. A "unifying look" is a function of format continuity, a topic I will cover extensively in just a moment. A "unifying point of view" is a matter of substance (content) and is founded in the presentation's objective, outline, and storyboard. If you follow the 10 Rules of Power Pitching your point of view is 20-20. If you don't, your point of view could be pointless.

One way to help drive home your point of view is to title your presentation. Titles lend a professional edge to business presentations. The title should be as specific to the presentation objective as possible. For instance, meeting the audience's desires; zeroing in on a key service benefit or a unique or proprietary product feature; extolling a positive consequence of doing business with you. Themes should also include some of those action or hot-button words I spoke of earlier. I'm loathe to give examples because, as I just stated, a title should capture the spirit of the presentation being given. Generalizing can be misleading. Nevertheless, I'd like to show you some titles from sales presentations that will illustrate my point. Figure 4–3 (on page I-6 of the color insert) is a sampling of presentation titles that help establish direction and tone.

What I particularly like about titles is that they also help establish the presentation's look—the face of power pitching and our next subject of discussion.

4.4 FORMATTING: PROCEEDING IN AN ORDERLY FASHION

Formatting is the expression of the language of visual communications. Specifically, how text, symbols, charts, graphs, and images are organized, styled, and displayed on visual media. As you just learned, the visual impression principle directs us to format our presentations in a consistent fashion and in accordance with the design fundamentals of continuity, clarity, and impact. We'll term this *visual format continuity*.

Visual Format Continuity: Practical Guidelines

In the two faux Acme Fruit Juice Co. presentations we compared earlier, *all* the slides, in the literal sense, were formatted. The difference was format *continuity*. Visual format continuity is how you achieve a look of professionalism and make an unequivocal statement to customers or prospects that this presentation was engineered and built expressly for them.

Achieving visual format continuity isn't difficult. The guidelines are straightforward, logical, and easily executed:

1. Create and use grids to accommodate the display of text, symbols, charts, graphs, and images in a consistent manner.
2. Use colors in a consistent fashion.
3. Use a limited number of typefaces.
4. Use typefaces in a consistent fashion.
5. Images must be compatible with one another.
6. Keep image aspects consistent.

Now let's look at these guidelines in greater detail.

Grids: They Keep You in Line.

In graphic design terms, a grid is considered to be a system of coordinates used in locating the principal elements of a surface or series of surfaces. In simpler terms, a grid *defines* a format (the way the pages of a magazine look, for example). Creating visuals that conform to an established grid allow you to achieve consistency in the look of your presentation. Figures 4–4 and 4–5 are examples of design grids.

I have no wish to discuss grid theory with you. Nevertheless, you should possess a fundamental understanding of the need for and purpose of grids. Being knowledgeable about basic presentation design principles is imperative if you are to effectively generate (if that task befalls you) or evaluate visual output—your own or that of your creative resources.

(This is a good time to remind you that I will talk about the care and feeding of graphic designers, production artists, service bureaus, video producers, and other inhabitants of the creative community in the final chapter of this book.)

Choose a color palette and then use those colors in a consistent fashion.

Using colors in a consistent fashion will further enhance the continuity of your presentation. Limit your color palette to a background color, a color for your text, and highlight colors. As we discussed earlier, you can use other colors selectively to help make specific points or create various moods. Colors can also help you pace your presentation by differentiating sections or topics. For example, when you've been using a consistent color background or color combinations, a perceptible color change silently alerts the audience that you've shifted topics or changed direction. The more dramatic the color shift, the louder your "silent alert."

FIGURE 4–4

Book Grids

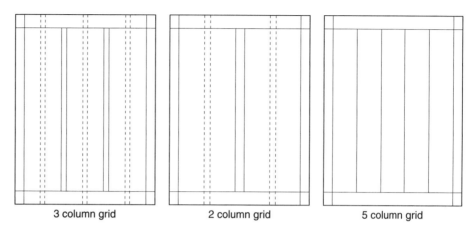

| 3 column grid | 2 column grid | 5 column grid |

FIGURE 4–5

A 35mm Slide Grid

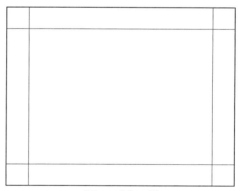

35mm slide grid

Your selection of colors can reinforce your presentation *tone*—significantly. If the tone of your presentation is bold and upbeat, you might opt for a color palette of primary colors (red, yellow, blue). If the tone is soft or breezy, pastels may be just the right choice. If you want to create a serious or clinical mood, dark, cool colors would be the ticket. The point is, color palette choice is not arbitrary; it should be a decision that takes into account your communications objective and the character of your presentation. Professionally, I occasionally use colors I personally don't care for but I know are right for the job at hand. That said, I'm reminded of a story that took place many years ago at Motorola. My boss's boss came by while I was working on a spring promotional event. He looked over the layouts that were on the conference table and said to me with no preamble whatsoever, "I *hate* green and yellow." Undaunted I replied, "I'm not that crazy about green and yellow either, but the art director at the agency who picked those colors knows a lot more about color than we do and these colors work well with our point-of-sale materials, and our dealers react positively to bright colors and . . ." He held up his hand as if to say "enough"; then he smiled and walked away shaking his head. Funny, but he never talked to me about color selection again.

Don't Use Every Typeface Ever Created Since Gutenberg.

Let's call this *typeface management*. Generally, one typeface is sufficient to support an entire presentation. Many designers like to use two typefaces, customarily one for headlines and a second for copy points. Of course, exceptions for emphasis or style are permitted. In fact, I encourage their use.

Apply Your Chosen Typefaces in a Consistent Fashion (i.e., size, weight, style) to Achieve Visual Continuity.

Graphic or visual designers keep the look of visuals consistent by developing type specifications (specs) for each project. Once again, you need to keep in mind there are as many ways to spec type as there are empty hangers in your closets (well, maybe not that many, but there are at least a million). Type specs are fairly straightforward and are usually expressed as follows:

Name of typeface

Point size

Weight

Style

Figure 4–6 represents sample designs for the type specs of this book and two other formats that were under consideration.

Images Should be Compatible Rather than Chaotic.

As you saw in the Acme Fruit Juice Co. example, presentations assembled from old, unrelated visuals can "perilize" your pitch—rob you of power. In that same light, images assembled from incompatible sources can also weaken your presentation. If the color values,

FIGURE 4-6

Sample Designs

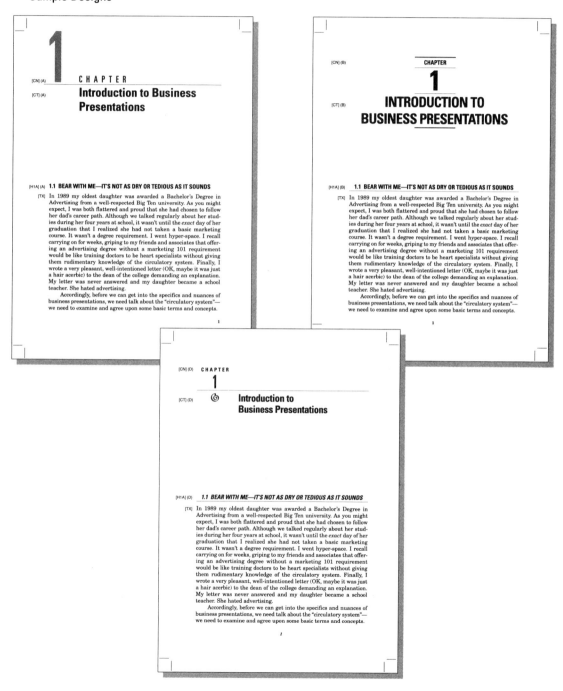

perspectives, or styles of photographs or illustrations vary too dramatically, they can distract your audience, or worse, possibly send out that dreaded "you're not important to me" message. But what if you don't have the time, budget, or even the need to create new illustrations or take new photographs? Stress not. Fortunately, formatting and photo processing techniques are available to help unify the look of your images. Let's use the four disparate photo images in Figure 4–7 (on page I-6 of the color insert) as an example.

Solution 1. We can format these photos (Figure 4–8 on page I-7 of the color insert) by carefully cropping them and applying them to a grid. Formatting is usually all that's needed to solve the problem. (In fact, when it comes to illustrations, it's often the only way.)

Solution 2. Photographs and (occasionally) illustrations can be "processed" to help achieve a unified, stylized presentation look. Photo processing has been around for a long time, but digital technology has made it easier and less costly, in addition to offering more variations and options than ever before. Scan in an old photo, tweak a mouse, hit a few command keys, and voilá—you have art. Figure 4–9 (on page I-7 of the color insert) provides some examples of processing or finishing techniques.

If at all possible, be sure your visuals maintain a constant aspect or orientation (e.g., slide orientation should be all vertical or all horizontal; boards should be the same size and orientation).

Is there anything more annoying than popping up a slide that's half on the screen and half on the ceiling? Fumbling around with boards, overheads, slides, or any other means of visual support is distracting to both you and your audience. You look like a goof; you feel like a goof.

As is often the case, the best way to *avoid* this annoying problem is with proper planning and sufficient lead time. However, there will be those inevitable times when you are stuck with visuals of different sizes, types, or orientations. When that occurs, you *must* devote some rehearsal time to getting comfortable with your visual support—you don't want anything to disrupt your presentation's rhythm or flow. If you're forced to use a mix of vertical and horizontal slides, the best worst case is to adjust the slide projector to accommodate the vertically oriented slides. The horizontal slides may look like they're floating (if you've ever seen a CinemaScope movie aired on AMC, you know precisely what I mean by "floating"), but it sure beats asking your audience to *read the floor* while you're trying to convince them how well organized, competent, and sophisticated you are. (Here's a thought. When you've finished the presentation, lose the slides.)

Use This Checklist to Ensure Visual Format Continuity

So now, in addition to evaluating your visuals for clarity, comprehension, and impact, you must also be sure your presentation makes a positive visual impression. This checklist summarizes the practical guidelines for achieving visual format continuity:

❑ Grid structure
  Are text, symbols, charts, graphs, and images displayed in a consistent fashion, and do they have a unified appearance?

❑ Color palette
  Is your color palette limited to a background color, a color for your text, and highlight colors?

❑ Typefaces
  Does the main body of your visuals feature no more than two typefaces?

❑ Type styling
  Are typefaces consistent in size, weight, and character?

❑ Images
  Have you displayed photographs and illustrations in a consistent fashion, and / or do they have a unified look?

❑ Aspect
  Are your visuals the same size and / or orientation?

4.5 PRESENTATION MODULES: SOMETIMES THE PART IS GREATER THAN THE WHOLE

Of all the enhancements you can affect to make your presentation more memorable, arguably none is more powerful than a presentation module. Now, before I go on, I must explain that *module* is an industry term (jargon) that broadly refers to a "specially produced audiovisual presentation segment." Think of modules as mini-presentations, or presentations within the presentation. Their purpose is to add depth to key points or issues, stimulate interest, or reinforce conclusions. All primary presentation media, and most supporting presentation media, can be used to create modules. You should also recognize that *videos are always modules.* I'll discuss this important distinction in enthralling detail in Chapter 6.

Module Classifications and Categories

Audiovisual presentation modules fall under two broad classifications: conceptual and didactic. *Conceptual modules* are directed to the emotional sensibilities of an audience and are distinguished by their use of images and (often) soundtracks of music and/or dialogue. *Didactic modules,* on the other hand, are directed to the intellect of the audience and are instructive or informational in nature. (They may also include images and have a soundtrack.)

For the purposes of this discussion, I've broken modules into four general categories: traditional opening, traditional closing, universal, and segue. Regardless of content, media, or production values, virtually all modules can be conceptual or didactic and fall into one of these four categories. Understanding the differences among module types will help you decide when, where and how to use them.

Traditional Opening Modules

I would compare traditional opening modules to musical overtures. They are broad overviews or "teasers" intended to gain attention, to serve as a prelude of what's ahead, and to get the audience in the proper frame of mood to be receptive to what they're about to hear. Traditional opening modules are almost always preproduced and have a voice and/or music track supporting the visuals. Under the right circumstances, traditional opening modules can be very engaging and add a great deal of memorability to your presentation—especially if you customize the module to your customer or prospect.

Traditional Closing Modules

Closing modules are primarily used to help make a lasting or final impression on your audience. Traditional closing modules are presentation summaries *forcefully* highlighting the presentation's key points and conclusions. Traditional closing modules are particularly useful in presentations that cover a wide range of topics or issues. Often, a captivating, concise recap of all the reasons and benefits of doing business with you can be incredibly impressive. When you spend weeks putting together a sales presentation, you occasionally lose sight of the potency of your own arguments. I can honestly recall several instances where I prepared closing modules for presentations of that sort and ended up impressing myself. What a great way to develop confidence going into a pitch.

Universal Modules

Universal modules are so named because they can open, close, or stand in the middle of a presentation. I've divided universal modules into five subcategories: bias-busting, empathetic, singular reinforcement, distinguishing, and in-depth. Each has a specific purpose and role to play in a business presentation.

Bias-Busting Modules When you are aware of a hidden or overt objection, sometimes the best strategy is to face it head on. Using a sales presentation example, let's suppose you learn your customer or prospect believes that your organization is too small, too inexperienced, too rigid, or ill equipped to handle the assignment, contract, or project you're pitching. A dramatic, fact-rich module that gives evidence of the size, experience, flexibility, or expertise of your company might be just the right tactic to overcome that objection. One caution. Bias-busting modules must be carefully crafted to avoid looking like a contrivance or an apologia. There is a fine line between understating and overstating your case. Consequently, if you plan to use this type of module in your presentation, my advice is to work with a qualified professional resource to help create and produce it.

Empathetic Modules Empathetic modules are a terrific way to generate interest in your presentations as well as gain respect from your audience. The Abbott HomeCare video I cited earlier, which discussed the problems hospitals were facing due to changes in the marketplace and then offered a hopeful solution, is a prime example of an empathetic module. In almost every case, the Abbott salesperson was able to proceed from that module (it opened the meeting) with a rapt audience eager to learn more. More often than not, empathetic modules are didactic. Therefore, as a presenter, you must be able to back up your facts, figures, and conclusions should they be challenged. So don't exaggerate or fantasize; it could be hazardous to your wealth.

Singular Reinforcement Modules Singular reinforcement modules address only the key point or conclusion of your presentation. For instance, if you believe that quality control is the most important criterion your customer or prospect will consider in making the purchase decision, then it's not too much of a stretch to conclude that a module devoted to the virtues and strengths of your QC program could provide the impetus needed to win the business.

Distinguishing Modules   A distinguishing module is a positioning strategy that is based on *unique* organizational strengths or accomplishments. The intention of this module is to distinguish your company from its competitors. If your company built the engine that sent the first rocket to the moon or developed a breakthrough drug or invented technology that significantly altered the course of the way people do business or founded a new system or procedure for managing a specific task, then a module that calls attention to that feat may be highly desirable. But take counsel; you really need to think long and hard about creating and using distinguishing modules. If the modules are not carefully produced, you can come off as arrogant or possibly even leave the audience thinking, That's nice, so what have you done lately? (I am reminded of a company that's still around, but not very well known, AMI corporation. AMI pioneered what we term photocopying somewhere in the 1960s, but gave up its leadership to a young, aggressive company named Xerox. I would doubt that very many AMI salespeople talk about their pioneering of xerography very often.)

In-Depth Modules   Although they can be constructed in a variety of ways, in-depth modules have one primary goal—to provide comprehensive coverage of a particular issue or subject. Typically, the goal of this type of module is to impress your audience with the depth and breadth of your knowledge about a given topic. But be careful not to get so detailed that you lose or bore your audience. Refer to your audience analysis: If you feel that some members of your audience already know some of the information you're covering, acknowledge that fact and then try to spend as little time as possible covering that material (or better, try to brighten it up with your visuals or insights).

To add interest to in-depth modules, I often follow the magazine feature-story model of including one or two sidebar stories. This tactic can be a very effective. A good example of a sidebar is a sales presentation we helped put together for the Middleby Marshall Company. One of its key products is a conveyor oven that revolutionized the restaurant pizza marketplace when it was first introduced in the 1980s. It even became known as the "pizza" oven because it allowed the big pizza chains to "guarantee" lunch or delivery in a fixed time (or the pizza was free—you may recall the hype). In fact, the oven was a whole lot more than a pizza oven. The company's then marketing director, Craig Wilson, hired us to help his distribution resources get that message out. Seafood restaurants were a prime target because several well-known local chains were using the Middleby oven with remarkable success. We opted to create a testimonial module (on video) and recommended, since we were taping in Florida, adding a sidebar story on commercial deep-sea fishing and packing. We based this recommendation on Middleby's perceived need to gain respect as a market-savvy equipment supplier by seafood purveyors. After the video was produced and released, reports from the field came pouring in that seafood restaurant operators were as enthralled with the fishing story as they were with the oven story. Almost overnight, Middleby became a seafood expert and its oven, in some circles, became known as the "seafood" oven. Wilson loved it.

Segue Modules

Segue modules are used primarily to change the tone or direction of your presentation. They are usually brief but emphatic—your audience will most certainly know you're about to change the tone or direction of your presentation.

Segue modules are ideal for introducing a new (expert) presenter. Let's go back to our singular reinforcement module example in which we believed the need to reinforce QC was paramount. Suppose you had the option of having the head of your QC department meet with and answer questions from your audience and decided that would be more beneficial to your presentation than a QC module. A segue module could overview your quality control operation and then serve to introduce the QC speaker. Very professional.

What if you've just gone through quite a bit of critical, but nevertheless, dry, technical, data, and you need to enliven your presentation. A segue module can immediately create a more upbeat mood and perfectly set up the next section of your presentation. Very professional.

You can help the pacing and add interest to long, sectionalized presentations by creating a series of segue modules to use as transitions between presentation segments. Very professional.

Customizing Modules

Most modules are easy to customize; all that's usually required is to add your audience's name to the visuals in the appropriate places and your mission is accomplished. Similarly, you can customize canned modules by adding a few visuals that feature your audience's name, logo, products, retail outlets, factories, people, trucks, or any other relevant symbol or image. Usually, a customized module can make the entire presentation feel customized.

One of the most creative and effective customized modules I ever produced was for Quaker Oats. We were hired to create a three-part opening module that was targeted to major fast-food restaurants, family restaurants, and hotel chains. The opening module had two objectives: (1) to create awareness of the huge number of brands Quaker marketed and (2) to underscore Quaker's commitment of people and resources to its customers. It was a huge project: weeks of preproduction activities, seven days of taping, two weeks of editing, computer animation, and original music. The first section artfully covered Quaker's broad array of products; the second section highlighted Quaker's organizational strengths and capabilities; the final section, which set up the subsequent live presentation, discussed commitment and was supported by a song we wrote titled "Quaker and You." In addition to including the name of the customer or prospect on the opening and closing presentation titles, we left holes in the final section that allowed us (in editing) to create the impression that this video was produced specifically for the target customer or prospect being pitched. For example, we could insert Quaker executives looking over the target company's annual report, R&D people examining the customer's or prospect's food products, and exterior views or interior shots of Quaker people dining at the target restaurant or hotel. We ended the video with a group shot of Quaker people toasting the customer or prospect (with Gatorade, of course), using cups featuring the customer's or prospect's logo. The real beauty of this upbeat, informative, entertaining opener was the fact that it could be customized quickly (half-day shoot/half-day edit) and was very cost-effective.

Using and Producing Modules for Fun and Profit

Determining where, or even if, to use a module includes both subjective and objective considerations. Subjectively, you can determine the desirability of creating a module by reexamining your presentation objective, your relationship with the customer or prospect, the nature of the audience, the venue, and the tone and structure of your sales presentation. Objectively, you must be sure you have the time, people, and budget to execute the module properly—especially if you want to create an elaborate slide show, electronic presentation, or video.

Suppose you decide that a customer testimonial video is a killer idea and would be an ideal presentation module. Well, you'd better know by now that you can't take your home video recorder, or hire your brother's cousin's neighbor who does cheap-while-you-wait videos as a sideline, and expect to end up with a professional-quality product. If you don't have the time or the resources to do the job right, either come up with another idea or drop the notion of a module completely.

Conceptualizing and producing audiovisual modules is similar to creating business presentations. For basic modules, *except* videos, you would follow these steps:

1. Determine your communications objective.
2. Develop a content outline.
3. Elaborate content.
4. Create a storyboard.
5. Select the presentation medium.
6. Produce.

For elaborate modules or videos, follow steps 1 through 3 and then plan to meet with a professional creative resource. Elaborate modules (like elaborate business presentations) are time-consuming and most often require professional creative and production support. Business and sales videos should *always* be professionally produced.

Power Presentations: An Advanced Studies Program

By now, you should have a solid grasp of the general principles and practices of power presentations. Consequently, if you apply these precepts to the planning and execution of your motivational presentations, you can rightfully expect to gain more business opportunities, close more deals, open more minds, and sell more goods, services, or ideas than you ever imagined.

To add to your understanding and execution of power presentation techniques, the concluding sections of this book are devoted to

+ A comprehensive overview of the primary presentation media.
+ A detailed discussion of videos—as I've already claimed, the most powerful marketing tool ever created.
+ Guidelines for effectively communicating with creative resources.

Beyond providing you with additional insights into visual presentation media, the concluding sections of this book are also intended to serve as a valuable reference that you can return to time and again to assist you in creating, producing, and delivering powerful presentations. Truthfully, if this book isn't dog-eared five years from now, I'll be crushed.

5
CHAPTER

Primary Presentation Media
Practical Insight and Unabashed Criticism

5.1 PRIMARY PRESENTATION MEDIA: THE GOOD, THE BAD, AND THE USELESS

It's the day of the presentation. You've were up late rehearsing, but you're not tired. In fact, you're pumping adrenaline—you're alert, eager, confident. You've done your homework, and you know your material cold. Your audience appears to be friendly and in a good frame of mind. The greetings, amenities, and small talk are winding down. Now all eyes are on you. You take a deep breath, smile, and . . .

I want to tell you that I have seen some very bright, well-prepared, well-organized presenters get flustered, lose control of their audience, break out into sweats, and generally go down in flames because of their choice of presentation media. Have I got your attention?

Boards, Formal Proposals, Overheads, Slides, Electronic Images— What's the Difference?

We've got some serious business to take care of in this section. I'm going to expand your knowledge and understanding of primary presentation media to make absolutely sure you select the medium (or media) best suited to achieve your presentation objective. I will discuss methodology for creating visuals (I promise to go easy on the techie talk). I will introduce you to service bureaus—those that specialize in presentation graphics (creative and production services) and those that strictly provide output (production). I will also reveal presentation techniques and strategies that will allow you to *maximize* the power of each presentation medium.

As I noted a moment earlier, I hope you'll consider this section a useful reference source and return to it as often as necessary. If you're already fairly knowledgeable about a particular medium, you may want to skim over some of the basics, but be sure to take a look at the application guidelines. You may find one or more of them helpful. Let's begin with the most fundamental of all presentation media—good old-fashioned boards.

5.2 PRESENTATION BOARDS: WARM, FUZZY, AND IN-YOUR-FACE

Presentation boards—low tech, unglamorous, occasionally a little awkward to handle—I love 'em. Presentation boards are my absolute favorite one-on-one or one-on-a-few presentation medium.

I got my advanced degree in boards at Earle Ludgin and Co. in the late 60s. My boss, Bob Pingrey, was one of the best in the business at pitching with presentation boards—in fact, he was a double-threat because he could hand letter like a pro. (In those days there were no practical photomechanical or other technological alternatives to creating boards.) When we were really under the gun, or had a major full-blown presentation to make, we would send our boards out to be professionally hand lettered. I can remember being totally awed by those boards when they came back to our shop—especially the charts. They were like pieces of art. But most of the time, Bob and I made our own boards. He forced me at Magic Marker point to spend hours and hours lettering and relettering boards until each passed his muster. After a while, I got pretty good at it. I also got pretty good at pitching with them. To this day, I still use boards to make presentations whenever possible. But I don't hand letter. (I ran into Bob Pingrey while I was doing some research on this book and asked him if he still likes to pitch with boards; "Absolutely!" was his reply. But he doesn't hand letter anymore either; too bad.) I'll tell you why I love boards so much in a moment, but first let me get you "board certified."

Making Boards in the 90s

Today, creating low-tech boards is a high-tech affair. Because of the pervasiveness of computers and presentation software in the workplace, the vast majority of visuals for application to boards are created digitally (i.e., converting computer files to printed visuals); however, direct transfer of visuals from reflective art ("flat art" as it's generally referred to by production resources) and photo processing are still viable.

The procedure is pretty straightforward. First, visual information and images are created on a computer, using a presentation software package (for a *very basic* presentation even word processing software will do the job). Then a hard copy of each visual is generated on "paper." The resultant hard copy may be further processed (enlarged or enhanced) before being mounted to poster board. Additionally, transparencies or flat art can be photocopied, photo processed, or scanned and printed to size and then mounted to boards. As I said, straightforward.

Let's take a look at the most common technologies for creating printed visuals. Please keep in mind this information is generalized— my goal is to *familiarize* you with these processes, not train you to operate the equipment. Your creative and production resources are normally on top of the technology and can counsel you as to which process or processes will best suit your presentation needs.

Standard Office Laser Printers (black and white/color)
A good quality printer that converts computer files to hard copy is the most direct method of creating presentation boards. Color printers are preferable because they allow visuals to be customized and enhanced in a more dramatic fashion. The largest size document a standard office laser printer can output is 8½ inches by 11 inches, which is somewhat limiting. When larger boards are needed (often the case), alternative sources are required.

Standard Office Photocopiers (black and white/color)
Direct transfer and enlargement of visuals to 11 inches by 17 inches can be accomplished on many standard office photocopiers; this size is quite adequate for most one-on-one or small group presentations.

High-End Professional Laser Printers (black and white/color)
Effectively the same as standard office laser printers but with an output capability to 11 inches by 17 inches.

High-End Professional Copiers/Printers (black and white/color)

Most common today on the high end are machines that can both copy and enlarge flat art as well as print computer files. The quality of the output of these units is surprisingly good. Output size varies; the largest I'm aware of is 22 inches by 33 inches.

Large Format Printers (poster machines)

These babies can make color or black-and-white posters big enough to cover an 18-wheeler. You'll probably never need a poster that big, but you never know. Currently, units offering widths to 55 inches and lengths to infinity (really) are available. The quality of large-format printers can vary greatly, so be sure you know what you're getting. It's always wise to see a sample if you're in doubt. At this writing a new technology is on the horizon (isn't there always?) that is touted to improve color quality at a reasonable cost.

Photographic Processing

For situations that require photographic images of optimal quality, photo processing is capable of delivering a beautiful image (assuming the original art or transparency is of good quality). Professional photo labs can enlarge your images to the required size. (You will be happiest with the quality if no text appears on the photo enlargement—the words will be fuzzy.) The enlarged prints are then mounted to poster board and can be used either on their own or in conjunction with your other boards.

Board Types

There are two basic styles of presentation boards: flip charts that are held together by a binder (usually an easel-backed ring binder that allows the presentation to stand on a desk or conference table) and freestanding boards that generally require the support of an easel. Both styles allow for customizing and are easy to revise, condense, or expand for subsequent presentations to the same, or different, audiences. Board size is limited to the extent it can be comfortably managed by the presenter—try to imagine flipping over or deftly handling a board that's 4 feet tall by 8 feet wide! Consequently, boards are usually not suitable for larger audiences—my rule of thumb is no bigger than a boardroom conference table. But the ultimate criterion is that every person in the audience must be able to easily read and understand the detail of the visuals. Let's look at these two styles of boards more closely.

Flip Charts

There is a fairly good selection of standard-size, multi-ring, easel-backed binders on the market. And like the old Model T, you can usually have any color you want, as long as it's black. Standard binders range in size from 8½ inches by 11 inches to 22 inches by 33 inches. Standard-size vinyl sleeves (which accommodate visual inserts) are also available—they make modifying or customizing a presentation a snap. The flip chart/sleeve system is especially helpful (as in saving your stomach lining) if you make a lot of presentations that need to be assembled at the 11th hour. Your office copier or laser printer, a nearby office support center (like Kinkos), or a professional service bureau can generate your visuals quickly (and usually) to acceptable quality standards—just slip them into sleeves, insert the new pages in the binder, and you're in the presentation business. Alert! If you elect to use a flip chart and sleeves for your presentation, *please* use good quality sleeves; they cost a little more but are well worth the price. Cheap sleeves crack, scratch easily, and, well frankly, look cheap.

As an alternative to sleeves, you can custom make your insert pages. Custom inserts take a little more time to prepare: You need to have the holes drilled, and the pages must be laminated to prevent them from getting grungy or shabby, particularly if you intend to use the presentation, or elements of the presentation, more than once. Aesthetically, I prefer customized laminated insert pages to sleeves, but only when it makes practical sense.

Binders can also be custom made to virtually any size, color, finish, or configuration you choose. (Obviously, if your binder is an off-standard size, you must also custom make your insert pages.) Binder covers can be silk screened, embossed, foil stamped or otherwise decorated to carry the message or image of your choice. I would encourage you to always decorate your cover; it enhances the professionalism of your presentation.

Freestanding Boards

Freestanding boards are not linked together in any way. They are usually stacked in order on an easel and revealed throughout the course of the presentation as required. You need to be sure your visuals are mounted on posterboard of sufficient weight to prevent bowing or warping. Aside from looking unprofessional, boards that bow are more difficult to handle—dropping or fumbling around with boards can be distracting, disruptive, and possibly worst of all, cause you to lose your rhythm.

In a similar vein, you already know that your boards should all be the same size and aspect ratio. But what if you need to create a larger board or display to properly show off an organizational scheme, a PERT chart, a distribution map, product samples, or the like? My preference (presentation venue and circumstances permitting) is to have that board or display set up and covered prior to the presentation; it can then be neatly revealed at the appropriate time. If circumstances don't permit a preset, keep the larger board or display separate from the core presentation until needed. In either case, be *sure to rehearse* your transition to the larger board or display.

Rehearsing the handling of presentation boards may seem like a small point, but let me tell you a worst case scenario I once sat through. I was attending a Sealy marketing committee meeting with several of my associates from the ad agency, reviewing new product ideas. One of Sealy's suppliers was talking about ticking (fabric used to cover mattresses) and had mounted different swatches on a huge board that he intended to display to the committee. It was obvious he hadn't rehearsed with it because, aside from wrestling it to the ground, he couldn't get it stay on the easel. After an embarrassing, apoplectic couple of minutes, he finally got it to stay up. But he was flustered; it was apparent his energy had waned. While trying to get back into his pitch he the nudged the board, causing it to fall off the easel and land on the conference table. Splat! Coffee and soda spilled on everything and everybody. I can still see Burt Goodman, Sealy's marketing and advertising VP, drenched with coffee and nearing rage. What a disaster. Do yourself a favor; remember this story the next time you think about *not* needing to rehearse the handling of your boards.

Using Boards the Right Way: It's a Love Affair

There isn't much I haven't pitched using boards: creative concepts, media plans, product plans, sales plans, employee benefits programs, financial performance reviews, research results, competitive analyses, and a few hundred new business presentations for good measure. Why do I love boards so much? I guess it's because I can touch and feel them—they really help me get involved with my presentation *and* my audience. I also value their flexibility: you can stage presentations ranging from serious, sober, and scholarly all the way to lavish, lively, and loopy. Here's what you can do with boards:

◆ *Look your audience right in the eye.*

Even if you've never read a book or taken a course on the subject of presentation techniques, you've undoubtedly heard about the virtues of good body language. Boards facilitate good body language because they allow you to make your presentation with the lights on. That means eye contact and—unless someone brought a magazine or a Gameboy to the meeting—the attention of the audience will be directed to *you*. Exactly what you want.

Speaking of people bringing magazines or other distractions to business presentations, here's my nominee for Rudest Presentee: New Business Category. Our firm had been invited to meet with a small medical devices company to present our capabilities and explore the possibility of working together on some upcoming projects. After being asked to wait in the reception area for almost an hour, we were invited into the marketing honcho's office. He was on the phone when we entered his office, but he motioned for us to sit down at a cluttered, small round conference table off in the corner. He finished his call but remained at his desk, which was about 15 feet or so away from us. One of my associates (who knew this guy) began the meeting with predictable arcane industry small talk. I noted that the presentee seemed to be occupied with some sort of paperwork. Finally, we were ready to begin our "formal" presentation. I had a small table easel and several boards and samples to go through and asked him to join us at the table. He demurred, saying he could get the gist of it from where he sat. Reluctantly, I began. A few minutes into the presentation I picked up a sample and went over to show it to him. That's when I noticed the paperwork he kept diddling around with was his personal checkbook. The dork was paying bills! I turned to ice. I don't recall what I said, but I know I stopped my pitch at that point and sat down. I had no more to say. I'm not even sure how the meeting ended, but somehow my associate was able to wrap it up and we left. What I do remember is sitting in the car in the parking lot telling my associate through clenched teeth, "If I ever write a book . . ." I'm sure you have a nominee or two yourself. If you can top my story, let me know.

◆ *Get into your presentation—jump up and down if you like!*

Energy has a lot to do with the success of your presentation. Boards give you a lot freedom to be active. Typically, you're on your feet when you present with boards so you can really get into the presentation: You can create dramatic reveals; you can write on, paint on, or otherwise augment the boards; you can even pick them up and throw them (something I've done more than few times—with great success, I might add).

♦ *Build a communications highway.*

When you consider the ambiance (lights up) and the small audience (intimacy) that typifies this style of presentation, boards have a certain relaxing informality about them. Consequently, if you want your presentation to encourage questions and stimulate dialogue, you couldn't ask for a better setup.

5.3 FORMAL PROPOSALS: WHAT ARE THEY DOING HERE?!

To be perfectly honest, I've included formal proposals as a primary presentation medium under protest. True, they meet the established criteria for presentation media—indeed, they can carry data, symbols, or images that support a "live" presentation and can be utilized throughout an entire presentation. And, yes, I know many people like to make presentations with them (maybe because they put so much time and effort into creating the proposal they feel compelled to use them). But allow me to disabuse any notions you may have about formal proposals as a viable presentation medium.

Do You Often Talk to Yourself?

There you are sitting at a desk or conference table, or perhaps you're standing in front of a group. You've just passed out your formal proposals and are prepared to begin your presentation.

What's the first thing people will do when you hand them a proposal—even if you've politely asked them not to turn the page and get ahead of you? That's right, they'll turn the page and get ahead of you. I will guarantee you once that proposal leaves your hands, the audience's attention is no longer on you. You'll be talking to a bunch of heads buried in proposals, reading text, charts, tables, pictures, costs—how can they possibly be listening attentively to what you have to say? Any chance you had to set up your presentation, control the tempo of the meeting, or entertain questions on your terms have been vanquished. You have lost power.

I believe proposals should be passed out only after you've completed your presentation (using any of the other primary presentation media). That gives you the advantage of having the audience review material you've already had the opportunity to position or explain. That review may occur at the end of the presentation, or more commonly, at some time in the future. If you want to *literally* use the content of the formal proposal as visual support, then use boards, overheads, slides, or electronic images to selectively reveal data. However, I would argue that proposals and visual support for presentations are not one in the same—visual support, as it's designation implies, is intended to *support* an oral presentation. Written proposals are to be read and studied. It's like comparing apples and okra.

I'm sure there must be occasions where making a presentation from a formal proposal makes sense, but I've never run into one. In fact, if you take nothing else away from this book, I hope I've convinced you to never again use a formal proposal as a presentation medium.

5.4 OVERHEAD TRANSPARENCIES: THEY'RE NOT FOR EVERYONE

Click. The lights are off. Slam. The overhead transparency has just been gingerly placed on the projector. Squint. That often hard-to-read, odd-shaped quadrilateral on the wall is what the presenter wants you focus on. ZZZZ. Is anybody paying attention?

All right, so I'm exaggerating a little. But I do have mixed feelings about overheads. Admittedly, my bias is partially driven by the vast number of business meetings I have had to sit through, watching a seemingly endless parade of overheads drone by. (Happily, the lights were usually down low enough so I could doodle with impunity.) On the other hand, I've attended several presentations in which overheads were used quite successfully. Conclusion: Overheads *can* be a very effective presentation medium, but you must pick your spots carefully and use good technique. Before we delve into the subjects of application and technique, let's briefly talk about your options for creating and projecting overheads.

The Making of Overheads: A Film.

Overhead transparencies really began to grow in popularity and usage in the early 70s as advancements in the art of xerography allowed photocopiers to print on plain paper and other media such as acetate. Today, overheads can still be created from hard copy or flat art on photocopiers, but better quality overheads are created digitally.

Standard Digital Processing (black and white/color)

Standard output on acetate from a computer file is 300 to 600 dots per inch (dpi). The process is similar to creating a color photocopy. You will find the quality of standard processing quite satisfactory for visuals that feature simple charts and graphs or are created on light-colored backgrounds. Overheads are normally sleeved to protect them from dirt, scratching, and other abuses. Sleeving also allows the presenter to write on overheads (you can use special markers, but most standard markers or grease pencils work just as well) without damaging the original.

High-End Digital Processing (black and white/color)

High-end digital processing is a photographic process that requires equipment normally maintained by service bureaus. Output to acetate is of a higher resolution on this equipment (vis-à-vis standard processors) and is preferred for visuals displaying dark backgrounds, detailed charts, or scanned images—colors are richer; text, charts, and graphs are sharper. High-end overheads are frequently mounted in cardboard sleeves to prevent "fingerprinting" or otherwise soiling the film.

Do Projectors Really Make a Difference?

My personal view of overhead and slide projection equipment is that they are for the most part commodity items, although the higher-end models are more durable. My concern about overhead projectors is linked more closely to the technical delivery of the presentation. These are my personal operation guidelines:

1. Never make an *important* presentation with an old bulb. (I always relamp.)

2. Be familiar with the projector—know how to it set up, how it works. You want to project a "square," sharply focused picture.

3. Wherever possible, use your own equipment (*especially* for external audiences at off-site locations).

4. When giving a major presentation always have a back-up unit in good working condition with you and have new (fresh) bulbs handy at all times. Short of an act of God, there's no excuse for blowing a presentation because of an equipment or technical failure. One time we even outwitted an earthquake. Years ago our company was producing a critically important distributor meeting for one of our best clients. The meeting site was Mexico City. There were tons of slides and multimedia effects. Shortly before we left the States, my technical producer, Bernie Benjamin (one of the best I've ever worked with, a true techie-savant), suggested we spend an extra $50 for a battery back-up system. His reasoning: Mexico City is as notorious for tremors as it is for gastralgia. (You're right, it's a fancy word for Montezuma's revenge.) You can pretty much guess the rest of the story. Quake hits. Hotel goes black. Battery thingy kicks in. The presentation doesn't miss a beat. Our client loves us. I deify Bernie. It's a nice story. Just remember, *there's no excuse for blowing a presentation because of an equipment or technical failure.*

5. Rehearse with the overheads until you can take them off and put them on blindfolded. If you plan to write on the overheads, rehearse that too. Don't let simple mechanics disrupt your presentation. Look professional.

6. Be sure your projection screen is clean and not creased or torn. If you are forced to project on a wall surface, hope that it's bright and clean (but just in case I'd bring along a sponge and a bottle of 409).

Overheads: What's the Use?

I believe overheads are best suited for informal, internal presentations that are educational, instructional, or provocational in nature. They would not be my first choice for motivational presentations (sales presentations, in particular) because of the loss of audience "contact"—you must bring the lights down to properly display your visuals. I also am not fond of the rather primitive means of changing visuals and the overall quality of the projected image. All things being equal, I would choose slides, electronic images, or boards for *all external motivational presentations*. I would use overheads only if there were no alternatives (e.g., the audience you are presenting to requested that the presentation be given on overheads).

Please don't accuse me of overhead bashing (see "Formal Proposals" for bashing). As I iterated: Used properly, in the right type of presentation to the right audience, overheads are a terrific medium. Accordingly, unless otherwise stated, I'm going to restrict my comments regarding the creation and use of overheads to educational, instructional, or provocational presentations.

◆ *State your objectives at the onset of the meeting—get your audience involved.*

Your first overhead should clearly state the goals of your presentation. Expound on those goals and how you plan to achieve them. Audiences attending educational, instructional, or provocational presentations should know what you are trying to accomplish and what role they are expected to play (Can they interrupt whenever they want? Should they save questions and clarifications until the end? Do they wait for you to ask for questions? and so on).

♦ *Be certain your visuals are readable and intelligible.*

If ever the laws of clarity and comprehension needed to be rigidly obeyed, this is the time. Your goal is to effectively convey information, ideas, or techniques. If you're educating or instructing, be certain your visuals are carefully produced to help, rather than confuse, the audience.

♦ *If you're leading a provocational presentation do your homework.*

If a presenter (for no acceptable reason) is unprepared, or has obviously not thought through the material being presented, audience resentment can build rapidly. Members of the audience may feel their time is being wasted or trivialized. This is the biggest complaint I hear from attendees at these types of meetings. Use this opportunity to enhance your stature—don't risk your career or reputation by failing to take your responsibility seriously. (See Rule One.)

♦ *Be sure the visual image is sharply focused.*

In overhead presentations it's not uncommon for visuals to be on the screen for long periods of time. What could be more annoying than having to look at blurry, soft-focus text or charts for a couple of hours? I get a headache just thinking about it. Don't be a pain.

♦ *Verbosity is verboten: outline don't editorialize.*

Unless the purpose of your presentation is specifically intended to review lengthy documents, you don't want to dwell on pages and pages of text (especially in a darkened room). Outlines work better. Use them to move you through quickly to your key visuals (charts, graphs, tables, etc.). Your audience will be grateful and probably more responsive.

♦ *Do dwell on your key visuals: charts, graphs, tables, and diagrams look great on the big screen.*

Interpreting, analyzing, and discussing data or procedures is usually the heart of an educational, instructional, or provocational presentation. Good presenters like to review their key visuals in depth with the audience. Then they turn up the lights, pass out hard copy, and continue the discussion face-to-face. It's a great technique for keeping the audience involved and alert (not to mention awake).

♦ *Make your presentation more memorable by being picture perfect.*

Where appropriate, photographs can often energize your presentation—especially after long periods of reviewing detailed charts, diagrams, or illustrations. Suddenly, you can bring to life the concepts and ideas you've been discussing. Very powerful. (Be sure to use high-end processing to capture the detail and richness of the original photographs or transparencies.)

♦ *It's even OK to joke around.*

Because many educational, instructional, or provocational presentations are dry, humor is often a good device to keep the audience alert and interested. Customized cartoons or amusing captions attached to otherwise innocent photos (à la the "Saturday Night Live" news) often work well. As is always the case with humor be sure it is relevant, in good taste, and does not offend anyone. Or at least be careful who you offend!

5.5 SLIDES: THE BIG PICTURE

Winter, 1968. I made my first slide presentation to a group of Sealy Posturepedic licensees. I had come up with an idea for Sealy to sponsor an LPGA golf tournament, and the client loved it. It was to be a celebrity pro-am event similar in format to the Bob Hope Desert Classic on the men's tour. As an agency, we thought it would be a great promotional vehicle: all kinds of merchandising opportunities; pro-am slots for selected customers; newsworthiness (the tournament would offer the largest purse in LPGA history); and the icing on the cake—a network to telecast the event. The Sealy LPGA Classic (as it was to be called) was my baby, and I was eager to get the Sealy people excited. Although I had never presented with slides before I was sure it was no big deal. Burt Goodman (you remember him, Mr. Coffee Pants), was an experienced slide presenter and tried to help me get my act together. Unfortunately, I never heard a word he said. Who needs experience when you've got youthful exuberance? Now I'm sure you're expecting me to tell you how terrible I was and what a disaster the presentation was. Well actually, *I* didn't think the presentation went badly at all—the idea itself, in concert with all the advertising and promotional support carried the day. The audience loved the idea. Burt was happy because the audience was happy. Then I saw Bob Pingrey, and he wasn't smiling. On his scorecard my slides were out of synch; they were on too long, they were confusing, and I tried to be funny and bombed. He told me I had embarrassed myself and the agency. I was abashed. But in hindsight, Bob (once again) did me a huge favor—he made me take stock of myself; he made me realize that it takes discipline and hard work to stand out from mediocrity. I vowed I would never make another lame presentation again.

From that day forward I made a study of presenters and their use (or misuse) of visual support. I inventoried what worked, and just as importantly, what did not. (For the record, the absolute best business presenter I have ever seen is Bob Galvin, long-time chairman of Motorola and still an active force.) Some would call my eventual cofounding of a marketing communications firm in the mid-70s, offering a distinctive competence in business presentations, an overreaction. Maybe so. But the fact remains I've created an awful lot of slide presentations in my lifetime, and I know how use them to their best advantage.

Where Do Slides Come From?

Before I tell you how to use slides to *your* best advantage, we should discuss slide production. As much as I'd like tell you all about how slides used to be made in the "old days" (the 80s!) using camera stands and mixing dyes, I'll spare you. Today, most slides are created on computer files using presentation software packages. The 35mm slides are then made in-house or sent to service bureaus for processing. (Service bureaus specializing in presentation graphics can also create the files from your storyboards.) Other slides may be generated from flat art or by photography (e.g., photos of physical locations, people, products). Moreover, duplication of individual slides or complete programs is relatively fast and inexpensive. All in all, slide production is a fairly simple, direct process.

Be Nice to Your Service Bureau

I think this is a good time to talk briefly about service bureaus—companies that specialize in the creation and production, or just the production (output), of presentation visuals. New technology has put most of the big slide houses and multimedia production companies out to pasture. Those that survived have gone into video production or become service bureaus. Your service bureau should be viewed as an important member of your presentation team. If you are like most of us, you'll have your share of 11th-hour changes, additions, and second thoughts (sometimes even first thoughts). A good service bureau (just like an in-house art or communications department) can make you a hero or break your heart. What makes a service bureau good?

Here is what I look for in a service bureau:

1. Good people chemistry.

The "service" in service bureau is all about people. I want to be sure the people I work with at a service bureau possess a value system compatible with my own and will take the time to understand my particular needs and idiosyncrasies.

2. Proactive involvement in my projects.

I want my service bureau to keep me from making mistakes, help me create better visuals—more cost effectively if possible. Whenever I think about that particular criterion, I'm always reminded of a printer I once worked with when my business was first getting off the ground. Sid was the nicest guy in the world, but he drove us nuts. His tour de force was the time he ran a stationery job for us. Our client called and told us the envelopes wouldn't seal properly. We called Sid. "Of course they won't seal properly; you can't print envelopes on that stock!" was his response. "Duh, why didn't you tell us that before you printed it?" was the best I could come up with. And just like the punch line of a bad joke he said, "'Cause you didn't ask." You don't need resources like Sid.

3. Their creative people can turn storyboards into exciting presentations.

I want to work with creative people who get excited about their work and get personally involved. I don't want to work with people who want me to make creative decisions—beware of "creative" people who say "pick a color" or "pick a border." I want to give direction and evaluate interpretation. More about this later (Chapter 7).

4. Their equipment is state-of-the art and regularly upgraded.

Top-grade equipment tells me they are committed to their business, which in turn means they're committed to my business.

5. They are technically proficient.

What good is great equipment if no one knows how to properly use it? Am I being hypocritical here? My wife wants to know why I had to spend $275 for a driver when I can't break 100. But I don't think it's quite the same thing.

6. They are responsive and reliable.

No further comment needed.

If you're presently working with a service bureau that meets the above criteria be thankful and take *them* to lunch tomorrow. If not, I suggest you try working with several different resources until you find a comfortable fit.

Projecting Slides: One Projector/Two Projectors/Three Projectors/More

The term *slide presentation* usually conjures up an image of someone standing at a lectern with a slide-changing device in hand, ka-chunking from one slide to the next. And I would agree. But slide presentations don't have to be that prosaic. You have a wonderful opportunity to add a dash of professionalism to slide presentations by using two, or even three projectors, which allow you to seamlessly dissolve or cut from one image to the next—always my preference whenever possible. For anything beyond one screen and three projectors, you need professional assistance—the design and production of "slide shows" (as the industry calls them) can be mind-boggling. I've produced slide presentations using as many as 24 slide projectors, and I'm aware of programs that have used more. (Relamping for those presentations is an event all by itself.)

One final piece of wisdom. It is generally assumed that you need to darken the room when projecting slides. Not necessarily. Rear-projected (RP) slide presentations can play with the lights up (as long as no light directly "washes" the screen), which can be an important consideration if you want to achieve eye contact, or if you want your audience to take notes, ask questions, or otherwise be involved in the presentation. Rear projection requires some special equipment. An audiovisual producer or any AV staging company can help you determine what you may need to stage an RP presentation.

Basic Operation Guidelines

Just as with overhead projector presentations, you should never make a major presentation with an old bulb or without a backup unit. You should also know how to change a bulb and what to do if a slide jams. For larger presentations you'll have tech support, which means all you have to worry about is your delivery.

Lenses, Slide Mounts, Trays, and One Other Pointer

As Andy Rooney might whine, "Have you ever noticed that little focus shift every time a new slide comes up on the screen, sometimes it keeps zooming in-and-out-and-in-and-out-and-in-and-out-and-in-and-out. Isn't that annoying? And why does it do that anyhow?" That "annoying" little focus shift is caused by AF (auto focus) lenses that adjust focus automatically as each slide is dropped. This shift is clearly acceptable for highlights of your vacation to Rapid City, but usually unacceptable for important business presentations. Without getting too technical, AF lenses find a spot on the slide and adjust accordingly. If the slide is out of focus, or the film is bowed or creased, the AF lens can go nuts. The best way to obviate the problem is to use glass-mounted slides. Glass mounts keep the film nice and flat so AF lenses usually stay quiet. They also help keep slides from getting dirty—slide film is a dirt magnet. Professionals usually use fixed, focal-length lenses and glass-mounted slides to avoid any possibility of a lens going whacko. I would always recommend using glass mounts. But they break, so be sure to keep a box of spares in the projector case.

While slide projector jamming is infrequent, it can happen. One way to cut down the odds of jamming is to not use trays that hold more than 80 slides. If your presentation requires more than 80 slides make a slide tray change (far less disruptive than a slide jam—often, the audience won't even notice).

Finally, if you intend to use one of those annoying laser pointers (call me Andy Rooney junior), *please* use it properly. In case you don't know them, here are the rules governing the proper use of annoying laser pointers:

1. Never point at the audience; you could inadvertently injure an eye.

2. Carefully point to the item on the slide you want your audience to note and then quickly turn off the pointer. Then continue your discourse.

3. Do not point to the item on the slide you want your audience to note and leave the pointer on while you continue your discourse unless you intentionally want to treat your audience to a laser light show.

4. Lose your laser pointer and forget to buy a new one.

How to Make Good Big Pictures

You can almost taste the food . . . hear the squeals of laughter . . . feel the surge of power . . . smell the noxious fumes. When it comes to visual quality, all other presentation media pale in comparison to slides. The picture resolution and color saturation of slides are such that every nuance of texture, tone, or shade is attainable. Text is crisp. Charts and graphs are vibrant. Images come to life.

Slides are very powerful visual communications tools. I want to guide you in their proper use. Please take notes.

♦ *Slides are your alter ego—make a good impression.*

Because most slide presentations are given in a darkened room, the audience's attention is on the screen, not on you. How important is that? Plenty. Be sure your slides look professional and meet the standards of good visual design.

♦ *Vary your pacing, but don't drag it out.*

You're sitting in a *darkened* room. The same slightly out-of-focus slide that says "Acme Body Tattoos Last Longer" has been on the screen for almost five minutes. Which phrase best describes what you are doing?

a. Listening raptly to every word the presenter is saying.

b. Dreaming about an exotic vacation with your lover.

c. Agonizing over the easy shot your partner missed last Saturday that cost you the club doubles championship.

d. Revising your to-do list.

If you answered *a,* go back to the beginning of the book and try again. To keep your audience invested in your presentation, you must hold their attention. (Remember, they're not looking at you.) One way to keep their interest is to regularly offer new visuals. My minimum is 4:1 (four slides per minute), and I prefer 6:1. At 4:1, you're changing visuals (on average) every 15 seconds, an acceptable rate. But be careful. If you rigidly adhere to a slide change every 10 or 15 seconds, your presentation (unless it's very brief) can become predictable and monotonous—your audience may tune you out. Consciously plan to include some rapid-fire visuals or add a few visual effects (e.g., slow dissolves, super impositions, abstractions that build to a recognizable image) or include a module in your presentation. What if you're forced to spend a great deal of time on a chart? Get creative. Cut away from the chart to a detail or show photos that relate to the data or put your inferences on a slide; you can come back to the original chart as often as necessary. Figure 5–1 (on page I–8 of the color insert) illustrates how this might be accomplished.

♦ *Cut down on fat.*

Consistent with not keeping slides on the screen for long periods of time, it's essential to *scrub your copy down to its essence.* Using key words or phrases allows you to visually reinforce your main point or conclusion; it helps you move through your narrative more efficiently. An equally compelling reason to be a copy minimalist is that text on slides can reach diminishing returns in a hurry, those little 35mm transparencies generally max out at about 8 to 10 lines of text. If heavy copy is unavoidable, try breaking it out into several slides. Sometimes more is better.

◆ *Think images not text.*

Images can strongly influence the way your audience sees your presentation; they direct the audience's imagination. Slide presentations thrive on images—no other presentation medium shows them off as well. Every time you supplant or amplify a text slide with a meaningful, good-quality image, your presentation gains power by more firmly seating the idea or strengthening the impression you are trying to make. But be careful; slides also make meaningless, poor-quality images even more meaningless and cheesy, negatively impacting your presentation. My best advice is to make every effort to incorporate as many relevant, good-quality images as practical into your slide presentation.

◆ *Customizing is a breeze.*

As we've discussed before, customizing presentation visuals is smart—customizing slides is not only smart but also easy and fast. But don't fool yourself into thinking you can just make a new title slide and then go party. Most of the time you're going to have to be a little more imaginative. You'll find plenty of personalizing opportunities within the presentation: Add a name, word, or reference to a text, chart, or graph slide; use a color scheme that the audience can readily identify with; show images that directly relate to or include the audience. Make your audience feel special.

◆ *Make your life easier.*

Beyond having exceptional visual power, computer technology has made the creation and production of slides about the most economical of the primary presentation media.

Slide presentations also travel well. Slide projectors are light weight, portable, rugged, and simple to set up and operate. Slides can be easily carried in trays or in sleeves. And because slides and slide-projection equipment enjoy universal standards, matching equipment, formats, platforms, or software is a nonissue. Consequently, you can stage a slide presentation anywhere in the world (as long as you can find a willing audience and an outlet to plug in your projector).

5.6 ELECTRONIC IMAGES aka COMPUTERIZED PRESENTATIONS aka MULTIMEDIA: AN UNDERSTANDING

Are you blue because you have an underpowered microprocessor, lack operating systems that can accommodate digital video or high-quality sound, or suffer from outdated CD-ROM technology? Or don't you care? Or for that matter, do you have any idea what I'm talking about?

I'm going to depart somewhat from the format I've been loosely following in our discussion of primary presentation media to talk about electronic images. Electronic imaging—by far the fastest growing and sexiest of the primary presentation media—is also the most problematic. It's my view that this medium is going through it's own version of "information overload." There's an awful lot of software and hardware on the market with upgrades and new products coming on-stream everyday. Presenters (and presentation designers) barely have time to get comfortable or proficient using one program or format when all of a sudden, bam! They're confronted with a thousand newer, faster, better, cooler ways to make presentations more dynamic. It's dizzying.

Thankfully for us both, it's not my purpose or desire to analyze and evaluate software and hardware (that's why trade publications inhabit the planet). My mission is to provide you with a better understanding of this presentation medium and to help you use it to make more effective business presentations.

Help! I'm Drowning in a Sea of Information

It would be nice if electronic image presentations neatly fell into two or three general categories. Unfortunately, they don't. However, if you bear with me, I'm confident I can navigate us through this sea of platforms, icons, interfaces, and acronyms in order to help you determine the desirability and efficacy of this presentation media option. Step 1 of "Operation Life Jacket" begins with diving into the origins and growth of this medium and clarifying a few terms and concepts.

Creating and Displaying Electronic Image Presentations

I shall assume everyone reading this book at least knows that an *electronic image is created (authored) using a computer plus a presentation graphic software program*. The created image may be displayed on a PC or laptop screen. The image can also be projected to a large reflective (movie) screen using a liquid crystal display (LCD) panel and overhead projector, or an LCD projector. (When projected to a large screen, the room lights must be brought down. However, new digital light projectors are on the horizon.) If you didn't know that, fret not. By the time you finish reading the next several pages, you'll know more about this subject than 98 percent of your friends, relatives, and associates.

Presentation Software: Is There Anything It Can't Do?

The first generation of presentation software (e.g., Adobe Persuasion and PowerPoint to name two of the better known programs) was originally designed to facilitate the production and organization of proposals, overheads, and slides. Fundamentally, these programs allowed users to establish grids, build outlines, create charts and graphs, integrate text and images, and provide the tools to perform artistic enhancements (create colors, backgrounds, patterns, etc.). Many programs also offered segue effects (e.g., dissolves, wipes, irises) and have evolved to incorporate sound and motion, which are integral to multimedia presentations. Second-generation software packages (e.g., Astound, Action!, Director) were aimed squarely at the presentation market. They were marketed as multimedia tools from the outset and designed to merge text, animation, digital video, and high-quality audio and, most significantly, to facilitate interactive applications. Interactivity is one of the real strengths of this medium, as evidenced by much of the newer and upgraded application software.

The Virtues of Interactivity

Interactive means that audio and visuals can be randomly accessed on command (compare that to a slide presentation that is a linear presentation format). We need to consider interaction from two points of view: how it affects us as presenters, and how it affects a presentation audience. For convenience we'll term these distinctions presenter interactive and stand-alone interactive. *Presenter interactive* indicates that control of the visuals (or modules) rests with the person giving the presentation. The presenter has discretionary power to direct the content or flow of the presentation in response to overt or perceived audience influence. *Stand-alone interactive* refers to the audience's interaction with the presentation medium. The audience responds to prompts or menu choices offered on a viewing screen and is provided with the means to respond to those prompts or choices by using a full or modified keyboard. Given the focus of this book is on live business presentations, I do not intend to spend very much time discussing stand-alone interactive presentations (which can be superb teaching, training, or information tools—the trade show kiosk business is booming).

Production ABCs: Arduous, Burdensome, Complicated

Electronic image presentations can be produced on diskette, CD-ROM, or full-size laser disks. There is a tremendous difference among presentations created on these formats (especially when you realize that one CD-ROM holds information equivalent to 550 diskettes!). At first glance you might conclude that diskettes are very limiting. With respect to information, yes. With respect to electronic image presentations, not necessarily. For example, you could include a video module in a presentation that was created on a diskette by having the diskette cue a video deck to roll tape. In an instant, your audience is viewing full-motion video. (I don't want to mislead you, it's not quite as simple as I'm making it sound, but it is very doable.) I could go on for days discussing all sorts of creation and production variations and permutations. But again, that's not my purpose or desire. *My purpose is to caution you that regardless of what anyone may claim to the contrary, creating good quality computer presentations is not easy.* In truth, most electronic image presentations are really the domain of professional presentation designers (especially if they're of the interactive variety). Having said that, I will concede that you probably could create a simple multimedia presentation if you met the following criteria:

1. You have good computer skills.
2. You possess a good hands-on working knowledge of a presentation software program.
3. You have adequate time.
4. You truly enjoy the creative process.

But even if you can meet these criteria, is creating visuals something you really want to do? Is it the best use of your time? I sure hope the vast majority of you responded, "Absolutely not!" to one or both of those questions. (On the other hand, if you answered, "You bet!" then you should probably be reading a different book and subscribing to *Multimedia Producer* or *AV Video* magazine.)

Winnowing down the Many Faces of Electronic Images

After much deliberation and consultation with "people in the business," I have developed six general categories of electronic image presentations:

Enhanced slide presentations.

Multimedia presentations.

Presenter interactive enhanced slide presentations.

Presenter interactive multimedia presentations.

Stand-alone interactive enhanced slide presentations.

Stand-alone interactive multimedia presentations.

Allow me to briefly qualify the six general categories of electronic image presentations:

1. Enhanced Slide Presentations

Presentations that feature electronic images with limited motion and effects but *without* video or audio are classified as *enhanced slide presentations*. At their most basic, electronic images are slides or overheads with limited motion.

2. Multimedia Presentations

Presentations that incorporate electronic images *plus* digital video or sound are designated as *multimedia presentations*. Consequently, by our definition, an enhanced slide presentation that incorporates audio *or* video would be classified a multimedia presentation.

3. Presenter Interactive Enhanced Slide Presentations

Presentations that feature electronic images with limited motion and effects (no video or audio) and are interactive, with control resting in the hands of the presenter, would be termed *presenter interactive enhanced slide presentations*.

4. Presenter Interactive Multimedia Presentations

Presentations that include electronic images *plus* digital video or sound and are interactive, with control resting in the hands of the presenter, are classified as *presenter interactive multimedia presentations*.

5. Stand-Alone Interactive Enhanced Slide Presentations

Presentations that feature electronic images with limited motion and effects (no video or audio), are interactive, and interface directly with audiences would be termed *stand-alone interactive enhanced slide presentations*.

6. Stand-Alone Interactive Multimedia Presentations

Presentations that include electronic images *plus* digital video or sound, are interactive, and interface directly with audiences are classified as *stand-alone interactive multimedia presentations*.

As a presenter you are principally interested in enhanced slide presentations, multimedia presentations, and their interactive counterparts. What follows are general observations and guidelines to help you determine when and how to use electronic image presentations to accomplish your objectives.

Electronic Image Presentations: General Observations, Biases, and Guidelines

Someday the picture quality, portability, ease of production, and lower cost will place electronic image presentations far ahead of the pack. In fact, there is already a well-established trend to using electronic image presentations for large-format meetings (audiences of 75 and over) that require visual support. Almost every major U.S. company is utilizing presentation software, to one extent another, for internal or external communications. Many have in-house capabilities. Even video tape will one day go the way of the eight-track. But for now, and the foreseeable future, you can expect change to be more evolutionary than revolutionary.

Now that the seas have calmed, let's see how computerized presentations can give you added presentation firepower.

♦ *Never lose sight of the fact that substance is still the name of the game.*

A shallow, unfocused presentation—even swathed in glitz—is still a shallow and unfocused presentation. Don't fool yourself into thinking you can fool your audience. Follow the 10 Rules of Power Pitching, and you'll never go wrong. Yes, I'm proselytizing.

♦ *Use the medium to its best advantage—let it enlighten and engage the audience.*

Bar charts grow. Text zooms in, out, and about. Colors are rich and vibrant; images provocative and fanciful. *Adding interest, conviction and memorability is the real power of electronic image–based presentations.* But there's a not-so-fine line between creativity and self-indulgence. It's a perilous line to cross. If you go too far and get caught up in the gimmickery and gee-whiz of the medium, you run the very real risk of losing your audience. Take this approach:

1. If points or conclusions are basic or self-evident, don't spend a lot of time and energy turning each visual into a cinematic epic.

2. Avoid using every device on the menu. Your presentation will lose it's rhythm and cohesiveness. It can also grow tedious (spinning pie charts and tumbling letters can get old real fast) and create a negative visual impression.

3. Pick your spots—direct your creative energies at driving home *key* points and conclusions.

♦ *Computerized presentations are great consolidators.*

Frequently your presentations will include input from multiple sources. The accounting department may furnish you with tables, charts, or graphs; engineering could send you technical drawings; corporate service departments might provide original art, archival photography, or vintage films. All input is welcome: It can be downloaded, translated, scanned, or otherwise integrated into your presentation. This is multimedia at its best.

♦ *Customization, modifications, and last minute changes are easily effected.*

Once the core presentation has been put together, making new titles, changing logos, and adding or deleting text or data—for the most part—are remarkably simple. You can literally make changes right up to the minute before you're ready to deliver your presentation.

♦ *Be a big hit at small meetings.*

Electronic image presentations are ideal for small, informal presentations played on a laptop or PC—especially because you can leave the lights on. It is the best of all worlds.

♦ *Seek professional counseling.*

No, I'm not talking about psychotherapy; I'm talking about creating computerized presentations. I believe it's important that presenters using this medium should be able to make nominal changes and modifications to their visuals. Frankly, it isn't that difficult. But when it comes to presentation design and production, I strongly urge you to deal with professionals. With good input from you, I can virtually guarantee that you'll end up with a terrific presentation and save yourself a lot of time and vexation.

♦ *If you sell high tech goods or services, act like it.*

This is by no means an inflexible rule, especially for internal or nonsales type presentation (computerized presentations can be costly). I think high-tech companies should make *major* presentations using electronic imaging technology. "Major" might mean shareholder meetings, presentations to the media or financial/market analysts, selected employee conferences (e.g., introducing a new benefits program), and key new business presentations. Similarly, companies selling sophisticated products or services that incorporate computer technology can make a favorable impression by utilizing sophisticated presentation tools. I am aware of one salesperson who uses a $10,000 computer system to project six visuals and run a short module. He sells a high-tech employee evaluation system. He's very successful. "It's showmanship," he happily claims.

◆ *Use the interactive feature (random access) to shape the relevance of your presentation.*

Let's say your audience is growing weary of the subject you are discussing and wants you to move on, but you've got 18 more slides to go through before you get to your next topic. Or suppose your audience would like to know more about a particular subject or issue you're covering, but for whatever reason, you failed to bring additional information with you. With presenter interactive presentations those problems can become opportunities. Push a button, and you've skipped to a new topic; push another button, and a menu offering a smorgasbord of data is yours for the feasting. What power.

Electronic imaging is still a somewhat nascent presentation medium, but its star is quickly rising. Your corporate communications department or a full-service service bureau can keep you up-to-date on the latest changes in software and presentation hardware. If you haven't used this medium yet, give it a try; it's not as hard to master as it may seem.

5.7 PRINCIPLE INTEREST

The creation and production techniques of the presentation media we've just discussed will continue to change and expand, but the principles I've outlined in this section are timeless. I hope you'll keep this book handy and refer to these principles from time to time (especially those of you who only make one or two presentations a year)—you'll be glad you did.

6

Video

The Most Powerful Presentation Medium of All

6.1 VIDEOS: THE MICHAEL JORDAN OF SUPPORT PRESENTATION MEDIA

I have seen new markets emerge for old products. Sales organizations driven to attain the unattainable. Distribution channels brought back from the dead. I have seen closed minds pried open. Complacency vanquished. Byzantine concepts simplified. Once, I saw a doctor embrace a salesperson and thank him for helping bring new hope to his patients. The power of video—it's enough to make a grown man cry.

I have been unrelenting in my acclaim of the power of video. Indeed, one of my motivations for writing this book was to help generate greater respect and appreciation for this medium. Inarguably, we are a visually driven society—television is inextricably woven into the fabric of our culture. Its power is profound. You've heard it before: Television influences the way we think, the way we speak, what we wear, how we look, when we go to bed. It is a populist tool that has inspired legislation and elected presidents. I would even argue that television played an integral role in the breakup the Soviet Union. Television ultimately became a window to the world for the Soviet citizens, a window that exposed the higher living standards of their World War II allies—and even more demoralizing—their World War II enemies. It was a window the communist apparatchiks could no longer drape shut, even with an iron curtain.

Given our nation's post–World War II predisposition to *visual* information and entertainment, and the pervasiveness (and portability) of videotape players and recorders, it's not surprising that video has grown to become an important business communications medium. But what is surprising, at least to me, is that most marketers seem to pay very little attention to content and production quality. Why is that?

Well, it's my view that the majority of people who are responsible for authorizing or overseeing the production of business videos are intimidated by this medium. Usually well-intentioned, they have no idea what it takes to make a good quality video—and even less of an idea about what a good quality video should cost. (I've been invited to bid on videos where crew travel and expenses alone would use up the dollars allocated for the entire project.) Let me assure you, when you finish reading this chapter, you'll know what it takes to make good a quality video—and what it should cost.

Before we move forward, I want to be certain you understand that the term *video* is *not* synonymous with "videotape." *Videotape* is a production medium that captures and plays back pictures and sound. *Videos* are a communications medium (just as film is a *production* medium, and movies are a *communications* medium). Videos can accommodate all the elements of the visual language plus incorporate full-motion images and audio tracks (music, dialogue, narration, sound effects). A video can contain videotape footage, film footage, still photography, illustrations, computer generated animation . . . the list is endless.

Those of you who are responsible for the creation and production of major marketing and sales presentations are, like it or not, "executive producers." Executive producers wield a lot of power: They control the purse strings; hire the writers, producers, and directors; provide creative direction; and approve the final product.

I Want to Help All You Executive Producers Create Awesome Videos

I am going to depart somewhat from our broader discussion of visual support for business presentations in general and focus more narrowly on marketing and sales presentations. Specifically, I want to address *marketing videos*—videos created to help sell goods and services. One reason for this decision is that I'd likely drive us both nuts trying to qualify, differentiate among, and categorize the vast array of video styles and types that can be produced. (You can imagine just how *vast* with budgets ranging from several hundred dollars to several hundred thousand dollars.) But my most compelling reason for circumscribing this discussion is that *marketing* is the real strength of this medium—a strength I want to teach you to exploit.

We'll begin by discussing the character and advantages of marketing videos. Then we'll talk about how you go about determining if producing a marketing video is a good idea or a waste of resources. Next, if it is a good idea, we'll examine what to do first. And second. And third. And et cetera. We'll cover the subjects of hiring talent and production resources, relative talent and production costs, the video creative/production process, and finally, how to direct and evaluate creative output. I'm positive you'll find this material enlightening, interesting, and extremely useful.

Welcome to the world of show business.

6.2 MARKETING VIDEOS: POWERFUL MOTIVATORS

Instructional (training) videos are superb pre- and postselling support tools. Training videos targeted to *internal* audiences are used to impart product knowledge or improve selling skills. Training videos produced for *external* audiences often cover product application, assembly, or maintenance issues. But as a direct selling tool, marketers should be obsessed with *motivational videos.*

Motivational videos also address both internal and external audiences. Internally, you might want to produce a motivational video to rouse a sales organization to work more aggressively or to be more customer focused and service driven. But typically, *motivational videos are targeted to external audiences*—your customers and prospects—to help you win their business.

Marketing Video Basics

Good marketing videos enhance sales presentations; they do not *replace* salespeople. In fact, good salespeople love good videos. The very best marketing videos strategically "position" the presenter's organization and stimulate viewers to want to learn more about the product or service being sold—specifically, how that product or service can best suit their needs. These are the questions a well-prepared salesperson is champing at the bit to answer.

For the purposes of this book, a marketing video will be defined as follows: *any video that is motivational in nature, directly supports the sale of products or services, and is played for customers or prospects by sales or marketing representatives in support of a sales presentation.*

Let's talk about the advantages and strengths of marketing videos—some are obvious; some are not.

Obvious Strengths

1. Document feature and benefit claims.
2. Offer customer endorsements and testimonials.
3. Show off manufacturing processes, procedures, systems, or capital assets that would normally require customers or prospects to be physically on-site to observe.
4. Demonstrate (new) uses or applications for products and services.

In addition, video players require very little setup time and are easy to operate. Videos can be viewed in ambient light, which allows presenters to be more involved with their audiences (eye contact, body language). Videos are relatively easy to modify or customize and, under certain conditions, can be very effective leave-behinds. But there's more to videos than just the obvious.

Not So Obvious Strengths

1. As I noted earlier, the look and feel (net impression) of a marketing video makes a strong statement about the organization that produced it. Consequently, a professionally produced, interesting, informative, engaging program will always positively impact a sales presentation.
2. You can create empathy and build credibility by demonstrating the depth of your knowledge of a customer's or prospect's industry, operations, business climate, competitive situation, and the problems and opportunities he or she faces.
3. As an organization, you can better control the message the members of your sales and marketing organization present to your customers or prospects.
4. Repeated playings educate and enlighten salespeople, giving them more confidence in themselves and their presentations.

If you take a moment to consider the strengths of marketing videos, it's easy to understand why they have the *potential* to be so powerful. But, as I've already noted, that potential has been woefully underutilized. Perhaps the business community has been watching the wrong channel.

I can't help but wonder how many of you have actually seen a really good (and I'm talking *stark-raving* good), professionally produced marketing or sales video that's been thoughtfully integrated into a business presentation? Those videos are awesome—they reflect positively on the presenter and the presenter's organization as well as influencing opinion and motivating people to action. Contrast these videos with the "homemade" variety (videos written, produced, directed, and shot by product managers, ad managers, salespeople, senior associates, regular associates, junior associates, associate associates, and all other novices including wedding and bar mitzvah videographers) of which there is an abundance and that, as a rule, tend to be abysmal.

As Ross Perot might put it, stark-raving good, professionally produced marketing videos are the *only* kind of videos you ever want to create. Period. End of discussion. Next subject.

6.3 WHEN DO MARKETING VIDEOS MAKE SENSE?

By now, you should have a fairly good idea of the character and strengths of marketing videos. The obvious next step is determining whether or not a marketing video makes sense in the context of your presentation strategy and resources. That's easily accomplished by responding to the four questions posed by the following marketing video decision list.

Marketing Video Decision List

1. Will a marketing video help achieve the presentation objective?
2. Is producing a video a realistic presentation support option?
3. Can members of the sales organization be effectively trained and motivated to use this video in their sales presentations?
4. Are sufficient dollars and time available to produce a video that will reflect positively on you and your organization (quality production values)?

Now, we will examine each of these questions in depth.

Will a marketing video help achieve the presentation objective? Marketing videos are tactical in nature, which means they must be responsive to an established strategy. For example, the Acme Box Co.

has developed a new product that is *demonstrably* superior to competitive products now on the market. One of Acme's strategies is to launch a trial program targeted to its best customers. Clearly, a marketing video demonstrating product superiority would support that strategy. Taking another view, let's assume Acme has no new products to introduce but wants to increase market share by implementing a strategy based solely on price and terms. Since this strategy is driven by timeliness (i.e., minimizing competitive responses), telemarketing, direct mail, and support for personal sales calls with spec/price sheets would all be considered effective tactics. A video rattling off prices and terms would not be responsive to this strategy. It's difficult to generalize, but a marketing video would usually be responsive to strategies that called for one or more of the following:

- Offering testimonials or endorsements by "satisfied customers."
- Providing provable product or manufacturing superiority.
- Establishing verification of capabilities (expertise) or resources.
- Demonstrating product or service features and benefits.
- Explaining/illustrating highly technical or scientific subjects.
- Effectively communicating your organization's understanding of the customer's or prospect's business climate, operations, special requirements, etc.

Don't reject videos as a viable tactic because you think the products or services you're marketing are too basic or too well-known. Contrary to what the experts say, under proper conditions, *every* product or service can be successfully supported by a marketing video—even commodity products. I have seen and produced marketing videos for such ostensibly mundane and ordinary services and products as tablecloths, tomato juice, shampoo, soda crackers, frozen french fries, drop forging, clam chowder, and foodservice equipment and supply distribution. All incredibly successful because they supported well-thought-out strategies.

Is producing a video a realistic presentation support option? This question is easy to answer. Presenters must have the *time, means* and *opportunity* to include the video in the majority of their presentations (and for all key presentations) to justify producing a video. If they do not, producing a video is a waste of resources.

Can members of the sales organization be effectively trained and motivated to use marketing videos in their sales presentations? Arguably, motivated, well-trained salespeople can be productive with any sort of selling tool (even hand puppets). But the reality of any sales force is the bell-shaped curve: a few outstanding salespeople, a few marginal ones, and the balance somewhere in between. Therefore, thoughtfully created, powerful sales-support materials can make a tremendous impact on the efficacy of a sales organization—this is especially true for marketing videos, but salespeople must be trained and motivated to use them effectively.

How often are sales-support materials—anything from simple ad specialties like pens and coffee mugs to elaborate brochures and slide presentations—dumped on the heads of salespeople with little more than a "go get 'em tiger" cover note? Pens, mugs, hats, no big deal—it's tough to screw up a pen, mug, or hat. But brochures, slides, and videos are another matter. They require explanation and direction: *why* they were was created; *what* questions or issues do they address; *how, when,* and *where* they should be used. The inherent danger in "dumping" videos is threefold:

- *They won't be used at all.*

Not being used might be the best worst thing that could happen. But losing the potential power of the video weakens your sales force and costs you sales opportunities.

- *They will be misused, negating their effectiveness.*

If salespeople are not given any direction or training with respect to the purpose of the video and the role it should play in the presentation (I am compelled to interrupt myself here and tell you that you can't imagine how frequently this occurs), organizations are then relying on their salespeople to figure out these things for themselves. Does that scare you?

- *They will similarly be dumped on customers and prospects.*

Absolutely the worst case. Assuming the customer or prospect does view the tape (not too likely), what happens when the video stimulates interest and provokes questions? Who's around to capitalize on that interest or answer those questions? Do the words *lost opportunity* come to mind? (By the way, a great way to give your competitors intelligence about your strengths, sales strategies, and business philosophies is to have tapes "dropped off" with customers and prospects.)

Finally, you must consider the comfort of the sales force with respect to the products or services they're selling and the people they're calling upon. For example, Acme Chemical's salespeople usually call on purchasing directors and occasionally manufacturing supervisors. But to sell a new solvent, created for use in the finishing process, Acme's marketing and sales executives are convinced that design engineers and quality control personnel are the key people to call on to promote trial of this new product. Acme's salespeople are anxious about making these calls because they feel "they don't talk the same language as those folks." They're afraid they won't be able to answer specific questions and will end up looking foolish. As a result, Acme needs to balance its salespeople's lack of confidence with a video that talks to design and quality people. By training and motivating its sales force to use this video, Acme will have a better chance of selling in its trial program, which in turn increases sales, which in turn builds confidence throughout the organization, which in turn expands the company's contact base with its present customers—which in turn makes everybody happy.

Are sufficient dollars and time available to produce a video that will reflect positively on you and your organization (quality production values)? Producing powerful marketing videos does not happen overnight. And they usually aren't cheap—at least when compared to the cost of typical informational videos or slides or overheads. Therefore, the risks are too great to try and get by with unrealistic budgets and time frames.

I had a client who understood this concept perfectly, and he had a great knack for getting me to "overproduce" his projects. Dick Shellenberger was vice president of marketing of the Syracuse China Corporation, a manufacturer of commercial china. Dick was one of the most brilliant and prepossessing people I have ever known. About every 18 months or so, he would introduce new products to the company's distributor principals at a high-level meeting, usually at a posh resort in Hawaii, the Caribbean, or Mexico. Oh, how I looked forward to those meetings. My usual responsibilities included creating speaker-support slides and video modules that helped position the company as the absolute, undisputed, total, and final authority in the market—which, by the way, they were.

By design, I created videos that had a character of objectivity and newsworthiness—a forthcoming discussion of customers, market trends, impending problems, and opportunities. But my videos were also designed to bring about a thirst for answers to all these eventuating challenges and tribulations, a thirst soon to be slaked by the company's sparkling fresh new products and robust marketing programs.

Dick and I worked together over a span of 15 years and never once failed to make quota.

Dick demanded quality. He maintained that quality was an *attitude*—an attitude that was reinforced by *performance* (products), *positive actions* (people) and *impressions* (communications). He believed that with all his heart. He used to say that he'd take care of products and people, but I had to help him with his company's image.

Dick always had tight budgets, but this never stopped him from wanting Frank Sinatra or Hootie and the Blowfish as an opening act. The first three times we worked together, he really got me. After a few input sessions, I'd develop a creative outline and some preliminary video treatments. (Treatments are like story lines; they often include sample narratives, dialogue, and visual ideas—we'll talk more about treatments in a moment.) "Don't worry about cost," he'd say, "just give me your best ideas." So I didn't, and I did. The ritual of torment would begin immediately after he approved the treatment and saw the budget. "Too high." So I'd prune out what was deemed least necessary and modify the treatments accordingly. "Too high." So I'd prune again. Eventually we'd reach nirvana. Then stuff started to slowly get put back in. "You know, we've got to have that shot of such and such in Detroit, or the point about upscale cafes won't really be understood," he might say; then he would quickly add, "Surely you're clever enough to get that in without increasing the budget." Ha! A challenge to my ingenuity. Then, later, "If we had that animation back in that *you* took out, the video would be so incredible that people would be talking about it for the rest of their lives." Ha! A challenge to my ego. Toward the end, when the pressure was excruciating, he might just say, cold as ice, "This has got to be in the video and that's that." Ha! An undisguised appeal to my fear of losing a client.

My most brutal meeting was meeting 3; I made about $800. But I got to go to Hawaii again and spend six glorious days and seven glorious nights in a hotel ballroom. Then I got smart. (You may wonder why it took this long, but you don't know Dick.) By the time the fourth meeting rolled around, I knew I had to hold back no matter what— "Come on Dick, add all the stuff you want." But it never happened. His product manager quit suddenly, and he had to devote practically all of his time to the product plan; he left the video modules to me. He told me I had earned his trust and respect. Then he looked me right in the eye and said, "I know you won't produce anything less than the best—anything you wouldn't be proud to have your name on—I know you won't let me down." Naturally, I went over my own budget. Ha!

After you've made the decision to produce a marketing video, it becomes *your* responsibility to make sure its message is on target, that it properly reflects the image and attitude of your organization, that it is interesting, and that it is sales-force friendly. You can do that.

In fact, I'll guarantee you can do that once you learn how to create powerful marketing videos. Ask Dick.

6.4 MAKING AWESOME VIDEOS: THE JOURNEY BEGINS

You've decided that producing a video makes good business sense, that it will contribute substantially to helping you achieve your sales or marketing target. Now what?

As executive producer, your *first* task is to hire an experienced video producer. Your producer will supervise the entire production all the way through to the final edit. As a rule, the producer will assemble a creative/production team including a writer, director, videographer, and production crew. In business video production, it's not uncommon for one person to wear several hats (e.g., writer/producer, videographer/director). The bigger and more complex the production, the bigger (and more expensive) the crew. *Experienced* executive producers sometimes hire a writer first (good writers are at a premium) and then bid the script out for production. They may hire the writer based on past (positive) experiences; or possibly because they were impressed by scripts or videos they read or saw representing the writer's skill; or they may have the time and interest to be more directly and personally involved in the video's development. In any event, preparing yourself to meet with producers or writers is where you begin.

How to Interview Producers

The best advice I can give you with respect to the interview process is to be as candid and responsive as possible. It will also help to remain open minded: Experienced marketing video producers will be able to help you create a more effective video *if* you allow them to share their experiences with you.

The key to the a successful interview is being *thorough* and *specific*. Offering direction that's vague and incomplete will result in proposals and bids that are similarly vague and incomplete (usually replete with a laundry list of assumptions, conditions, caveats, and disclaimers). On the other hand, providing precise, carefully considered direction greatly increases the likelihood of getting back thoughtful proposals and realistic bids. To be assured the direction you give is precise and considered you need to be able to articulate the following:

1. Marketing objective.
2. Presentation objective.
3. Audience profile.
4. Story line direction or ideas.
5. Use of the video (by the presenter in the presentation).
6. Video completion date.
7. Budget range.

Points 1 and 2 are familiar to you—you already know how to frame this information and why it's important for anyone working on the creation of the video to understand what you are trying to accomplish. Similarly, we've discussed point 3, the necessity of knowing the character of your presentation audience (to enable you to address the interests of attendees and properly influence their decisions). But we do need to briefly cover the balance of the list.

Story Line Direction or Ideas

Assuming the producer or writer truly understands your objectives (if he or she does not, I'd suggest eliminating that individual from consideration immediately), it would be helpful to also furnish some insight as to how you think the story could (or might) be told: a case history, customer testimonials, a day in the life of. You should be able to explain why you feel your story line or scene ideas would be effective. Good or bad, your concepts ultimately help producers or writers *visualize* your product's or service's strengths more clearly—it may even inspire them or lead them down creative paths they might not have otherwise traveled.

Use of the Video. (by the presenter in the presentation)

It's also important for the writer, and especially the producer, to have an idea of how you intend to use the video from a tactical point of view. Do you envision the video opening the presentation? Is it a module within the presentation? Does it close the presentation? (We discussed the virtues of each of these options in Chapter 4.) It's also necessary to determine if the video will serve as a leave-behind (leave-behind videos often need to be produced differently than presentation videos in order to compensate for the absence of a live presenter).

Video Completion Date

It's vitally important to establish a completion date. Your producer must be sure there is adequate time to properly prepare, shoot, and edit your video—the amount of detail and logistics involved in creating a professional video (as I'll soon detail) can be overwhelming. Be certain to pick a date that will allow you to have copies of the completed video in time to train the members of your sales and marketing organization in its proper use. Sales meetings are usually ideal for launching videos.

Be assured that experienced producers will be able to tell you if there will be any problems in meeting that date. (If the color drains from the producer's face during your meeting, you've probably got a problem.) The good news is that if there is a problem, those same experienced producers will usually be able to offer ideas as to how to meet your target date (usually without materially changing the content or impact of the video).

Budget Range

When someone would ask Don Wallace (my original partner, a technical whiz, and one of the finest producers I have ever known) how much a film or video would cost, he would always answer, "How long is a piece of string?" Video budgets are inherently difficult to pin down because the process is rife with *subjective* variables. Each producer you meet with will "see" the video in a different light. So just how long is a piece of string?

Fearlessly, I'm going to tackle the issue of cost head on. When I started this project I talked to several producers I know and asked them what they would consider to be the *minimum* cost of an "average" professionally produced video *excluding* script development and travel expenses—variables impossible to average. Since we could not agree on the definition of an average video, I established the following guidelines:

- ◆ Length is 10 to 15 minutes. (You should be aware of the fact that the length of a *finished* video ordinarily has very little impact on its cost.)

- ◆ A one-camera shoot with a three-person crew plus director, producer, make up/hair stylist, and production assistant.

- ◆ Three days of videography (location and studio, simple set construction, and propping).

- ◆ Professional talent (an announcer and three on-camera spokespersons).
- ◆ Editorial: two days off-line (not broadcast standard), two days on-line (broadcast standard).
- ◆ Stock music.
- ◆ A nominal amount of charts and graphs using two-dimensional animation and a character generator (as opposed to dimensional animation of the type seen at the opening of most sports telecasts à la the "Monday Night Football" crashing helmets—that type of animation runs about $1,000 per second).
- ◆ Location fees, tape stock, one day teleprompter, art work, and other miscellaneous costs.

Because I was intrigued with the results, I decided to contact a few more producers in different parts of the country and gave them the same criteria. Here are the official results of my unofficial survey: **$ 36,600.**

Survey Notes
The high figure was $55,000, the low $28,000. (I didn't participate, but my number would have been around $38,000, which would have put me just slightly over the average.) Several producers balked at using stock music; they insisted it had to be "sweetened" (enhancing stock music with original composition, usually synthesized). Others didn't like the mix of off- and on-line editing. But for the most part, all agreed the parameters I established were realistic.

I think this is a great starting point. You now have a real good idea of what professionals believe an average video should cost. The benchmark figure of $36,600 gives you some insight into the cost impact of additional (or fewer) shooting days or talent; more elaborate (or simpler) sets; more (or less) sophisticated graphics; and so on. I've reproduced a typical production bid sheet (Figure 6–1) to help you understand all the detail involved in video production—peruse this monster for a minute or two and you'll realize I'm not kidding when I talk about all the variables involved in video production. I believe this information will have even greater meaning for you after we talk more about the creative and production processes.

FIGURE 6–1

Bid Sheet Model

Bid Date:			Client:				
Producer:			Title:				
			Contact:				
Phone:			Phone:				
Fax:			Fax:				
SUMMARY OF ESTIMATED PRODUCTION COSTS							
					Estimate	Actual	Difference
Pre-Production & Wrap:				Total A			
Shooting Crew & Labor:				Total B			
Location & Travel Expenses:				Total C			
Props, Wardrobe:				Total D			
Studio & Set Construction:				Total E,F			
Equipment:				Total G			
Video Stock:				Total H			
Miscellaneous:				Total I			
			Sub-Total A-I:				
Creative Development:				Total J			
Production Insurance:							
			Sub-Total Direct Cost				
Production Fee:	25% of Sub-Total A-I Only						
Talent Costs:				Total K			
Post-Production Costs:				Total L			
			Grand Total				
Comments:							

FIGURE 6–1

(continued)

Crew: Pre-Pro & Wrap	Rate/Day	Days	O.T./hr	Hours	Estimate	Actual	Difference
Camera:							
Gaffer:							
Grip:							
Production Coordinator:							
Production Assistant:							
Stylist:							
Director:							
Producer:							
Research:							
Location Scout:							
Pre-Pro:							
Off-Line Edit:							
On-Line Edit:							
Wrap:							
		Subtotal A					
		PT/P&W					
		Total A					
Shooting Crew:	Rate/Day	Days	O.T./hr	Hours	Estimate	Actual	Difference
Producer:							
Assistant Producer:							
Director:							
Assistant Director:							
Camera:							
2nd Camera:							
Gaffer:							
Grip:							
Engineer:							
Electrician:							
Audio:							
Make-up:							
Stylist:							
Teleprompter Operator:							
Production Assistant:							
		Subtotal B					
		PT/P&W					
		Total B					

FIGURE 6–1

(continued)

Location Expenses:	Rate/Unit	Unit	OT/hrs	Hours	Estimate	Actual	Difference
Location Fees:							
Replacement Costs:							
Permits:							
Vehicle Rental:							
Parking, Tolls, Gas & Cab:							
Air Freight/Excess Baggage:							
Air fare:							
Sky Cap:							
	Rate/Unit	Unit		Crew	Estimate	Actual	Difference
Travel Days:							
Mileage:							
Per Diems:							
Hotel:							
Craft Services:							
		Subtotal C					
Props & Wardrobe:							
Prop Rental:							
Prop Purchase:							
Wardrobe Rental:							
Wardrobe Purchase:							
		Subtotal D					
Studio Rental:							
Rental for Build/Pre-Lite:							
Rental for Shoot:							
Rental for Strike:							
Crew Meals:							
Power Charge:							
Misc. Expenses/OT:							
		Subtotal E					
Set Construction:							
Set Designer:							
Props:							

F I G U R E 6–1

(continued)

		Subtotal F				
Equipment Rental:						
Camera, Lighting:						
2nd Camera:						
Audio:						
Lighting:						
Lighting/Grip Truck:						
Expendibles:						
Generator:						
Crane/Cherry Picker:						
Dolly:						
Monitor Batteries:						
Scan Converter/Walkies:						
		Subtotal G				
Videotape Stock	Rate/Roll		# of Rolls	Estimate	Actual	Difference
1" Stock:						
Betacam SP (30 min.):						
3/4 program dubs (30 min.):						
VHS program dubs/approval:						
Timecoded Window Dubs:						
		Subtotal H				
Miscellaneous	Rate	Unit				
Transcription:						
Parking/Taxi:						
Long Distance:						
Messenger/Overnight:						
Faxes/Copies:						
External Billing Costs:						
		Subtotal I				
Creative Development	Rate	Unit	OT	Hours	Estimate	Actual	Difference
Research:							
Scriptwriting:							

FIGURE 6-1

(concluded)

Storyboards:							
Producer:							
Director:							
		Subtotal J					
Talent							
VO Narrator:							
OC Narrator:							
OC Day Player:							
OC 1/2 Day Player:							
Extras:							
Signatory:							
Agent Fee:							
Pension & Welfare:							
FICA/Medi/Comp/FUTA/SUTA							
Wardrobe Fees:							
Handling Fees:							
		Subtotal K					

Post Production	Rate	Hours	Each	Min	Estimate	Actual	Difference
Off-Line Facility:							
Off-Line Master Stock:							
Window Dubbing Time:							
Record Narration:							
Audio Mix/Sweetening:							
Music Search:							
Needle Drop:							
Audio Stock:							
On-Line Facility:							
DVE:							
CG/Titles:							
Misc. a la Carte:							
Layoff time for dissolves:							
Master/Safety Stock:							
Layoff Stock (30 min. Beta):							
1" Boxes/Reels:							
Program Dubbing Time:							
Original Music Comp.:							
Computer Graphics:							
Stats/Slides/Illustrations:							
Stock Footage:							
Meals:							
OT:							
Misc.:							
Handling Fee:							
		Subtotal L					

Hiring the "Right" Video Producer

I truly believe there *is a best way* to determine whom you should hire to create and produce your video. Allow me to show you the way.

Given the budget model I just provided (be sure to allow for inflation if you happen to be reading this book 20 years after the publishing date), you should be able to calculate a realistic budget *range*. To the benchmark figure of $36,600, you can add or subtract dollars based on what you believe will be required to produce your video. Don't be intimidated or think small. (You know that additional shooting days or sexy animation is going to inflate your budget, so be generous in your "guesstimating.") You also need to allow for script development and travel costs. I wish I could help you more with estimating the cost of a script, but trying to come up with a hard figure is tough. Script-writing charges are a function of the experience of the writer, the complexity of the subject matter, how much research is necessary, and how much dialogue needs to be written. Most really good writers I know won't touch even a simple script for less than $3,500—and that figure is based on doing minimal research.

Determining a budget range is critical. First, if your budget-range estimate is light years away from your available dollars, you'll need to either find more money, scale down the video (if possible), or dump it. But if your estimated range is in line with your budget, you're ready to make a video. Keep in mind your objective is to *create the best video possible at a fair and reasonable price.*

It's depressing to me that so many marketing professionals (who should know better) look at promotional and marketing-support material as commodities and buy on price. Here's an example of what I mean. Back in the early 80s, I accompanied the president of a PR firm on a new-business presentation to South Carolina—the company we were calling on had something to do with home building and supply. Although I had done quite a bit of work for this PR firm, I had very little direct contact with its president. For lots of reasons, this meeting was like an out-of-body experience, not the least of which was that the prospect's marketing name was A.I.D.S. (I know the AIDS virus had been discovered and was gaining notoriety because I recall asking one of the principals if that acronym was troublesome to him; he looked at me like I was some sort of moron and blew me off.) But the highlight sound bite I want to play for you features the PR prez going off on why his firm should be hired. Listen closely: ". . . hell, *we* can do a brochure for $800!" Did you hear that! He didn't say,

". . . we can create a brochure that will really differentiate you in the marketplace" or ". . . we can create a brochure that will enhance your image" or ". . . we can create a brochure that will help you sell more products"—he said his firm could "do a brochure for $800." To him a brochure was just paper and ink—impression and content were irrelevant. It galled me to hear such nonsense come from the president of a fairly good-sized, well-respected PR agency. This man truly didn't get it. (He also didn't get the business. I'm not sure who was luckier.)

The Hiring Process by the Numbers

Do not begin the hiring process without having your production budget range in hand. Being in control of the budget allows you to go about selecting a producer for the right reasons—talent and experience (not who's cheapest). The process is logical and uncomplicated; I'll elaborate as I go along:

1. Find two, three, or at most, four qualified producers to interview for the project.

Unless you have nothing but time on your hands, you probably don't need to talk to more than three qualified producers. Underline the word *qualified* twice. Qualified producers aren't that difficult to find. Organizations that have produced impressive videos are an excellent resource. Call them. In all likelihood they'll be flattered by your request and eager to give you the name of the person or company who produced the video (or videos) you liked. If you have access to a full-service advertising agency, talk to the creative director or the head of the broadcast production department; one or the other should be able to give you the names of one or two qualified producers. Creative directories are also a good source for leads, but there is a bias. As a rule directories list names, phone numbers, and addresses by category (i.e., under subheads like production companies, writers, directors, photographers, etc.). Consequently, only producers who take out "ads" extolling their experience and expertise can be considered. (I suggest you remain a tad skeptical until proven differently—*anyone* can claim to be a video producer.)

To help you in the selection process you may wish to issue a request for qualifications (RFQ) to producers you feel merit consideration. Keep the RFQ simple and straightforward. Your objective is to cull out producers who either do not have the experience you're looking for or would not be able to take on the project and complete it in a timely fashion. Over the years, as much as I've disliked doing it, I have turned down projects because I honestly felt I couldn't devote the time and attention needed to deliver a high-quality product. Most video creative and production professionals share that philosophy.

Finally, for those of you who have been fortunate enough to have been involved in one or more successful video productions, I suggest you skip the interview process and hire the producer you know and can count on.

2. Begin the interview process by asking each producer to discuss his or her background and experience before you view a sample reel.

Your first step in the interview process is to *evaluate* the producer's experience. This evaluation can often be more subjective than objective—if you don't "feel comfortable" with the producer, don't fight your instinct; videos are very personal. Politely dismiss any producer you deem unqualified or unsatisfactory.

3. View each producer's sample reel with a critical and sophisticated eye.

A producer's reel is all telling. It's best to view the reel twice. The first time just sit back and garner a net impression. Again, trust your instincts. (Remember that the customers or prospects who view your video typically get to see it just *once*—making a good first impression is of paramount concern.) The second time you view the reel concentrate on asking business questions such as, What were the objectives of the videos and how did you accomplish them? Good producers usually anticipate these questions and often introduce each sample vignette with an overview of the project. Be wary of producers who focus on the technical side of video production or have trouble answering your questions.

A producer's reel can also be misleading. The most obvious features will be the production values—the visual quality of the video. You will more than likely be taken by the videography, the lighting, the graphics, and the editing. Qualitatively, what you see is what you can expect *your* video to look and feel like. That being the case, what you *really* want to know is whether the same people who were responsible for the videography, lighting, graphics, and editing you saw and liked in the sample reel be working on your video. This question is critical because many producers hire freelance writers, directors, videographers/cinematographers, and editors, and freelancers are not always available to start a new project. If a particular director's or writer's work stands out on the reel, and you want that director or writer, don't beat around the bush; insist upon it. In fact, make the awarding of the project contingent upon it.

4. Continue the evaluation process by talking about your business in general, the objective of the video, and how you intend to use it as a marketing or sales tool.

If you liked what you saw, you'll continue the interview by getting into some of the details of your project. Begin with an overview of your company—its operations, distribution, customers, competition, and so on. The producer should understand, generally, how your company operates and how it's positioned in the marketplace. Then briefly get into the specifics of the video: the current situation, your objectives, how the video will be used by your salespeople. Listen carefully to the questions the producer asks you. Are they good sound business questions, or are they naive or convoluted? Challenge the producer: Does this person really understand my business, my customers and what I'm trying to accomplish with this video? If the answer is no, or even I don't think so, you should again politely terminate the interview.

After you've completed the interview process, you have two options: (1) Offer the project to the producer you feel will do the best job, or (2) if you can't decide between or among the producers you've interviewed, you can ask each candidate to submit a creative treatment and proposed budget. It is standard industry practice for producers to charge for fully developed creative treatments *unless* they've been awarded the project; then there is no discrete charge for treatment development. Producers awarded projects without competitive bidding usually present several treatment ideas to their clients as a matter of course.

Regardless of which option you choose, you must next discuss the video in more depth: the audience, your story line ideas, and other issues that may impact the production of the video. You can expect the producers (or producer) to ask questions as well. The nature of those questions will give you added insight into how well the producer understands your project.

If you are selecting a producer based on experience, sample reel, or past history, by all means *reveal your budget range*. If you are requesting treatments and proposals, you have a choice. Personally, if I'm in a bid situation that requires a creative treatment, I prefer to know the budget range. Why? Because of all the variables and subjectivity I referred to earlier: One producer sees a particular scene being shot on a set, another sees it on location; one producer sees the need for a tight script and teleprompters, another feels it should be shot documentary style, unscripted. Providing a budget range ensures that a producer will come back to you with a concept that can be executed. Is there anything more frustrating than having a great concept and being unable to bring it to life?

In response to that interrogative, I decided to close this section on how to hire a producer with the Sunbeam story (the biggest disappointment of my professional life), even though it didn't involve a video production. It was the mid-80s, and Sunbeam, a manufacturer and marketer of small appliances, was making yet another comeback. It was about to launch a myriad of new and improved consumer small appliances. Executives were planning to hold a huge sales meeting in Miami to introduce these products to the sales organization. Selected producers were interviewed by Sunbeam's marketing staff, and a few were invited to return with creative ideas. We were one of the firms invited back. After days of trying to come up with *anything* but the trite big-multiple-screen-multimedia-musical-montage-light-show-orgy that I knew my competitors would propose, I was sure I had it! I remember getting to the office real early that morning so I could tell Liz Lucas, our account exec, my idea. As soon as she walked into the office, I pounced. "Who do you know who absolutely needs every single appliance Sunbeam makes?! Who! Who!" She jumped and stared at me speechlessly, her glasses alop. "I'll tell you who! Alice Kramden that's who! What an idea! What an idea!" I told her we'd recreate the old Jackie Gleason "Honeymooners" set and concoct a story about Ralph winning some money and surprising Alice by buying her every appliance she ever dreamed of (which, of course, would be all Sunbeams). The "big finish" would have Ralph plugging in all the appliances at once, causing an explosion and blacking out Manhattan. We'd hire actors to play the Ralph and Alice roles—maybe Ed and Trixie, too. And there was a kicker. Jackie Gleason lived outside of Miami. I had recently met the "Great One" at his golf tournament and knew "the right people" to influence him to go to the meeting. I planned to have Gleason on stage, first as Ralph (out of the dark, after the explosion) and then as himself at the end of the skit.

The salespeople would go nuts; it would be an experience they'd never forget. (Remember, the year was 1984 or 85, and the "Honeymooners" was still in heavy reruns all across the country.) Liz thought the idea was spectacular. And after it was honed and polished and budgeted, so did the members of the Sunbeam marketing staff. They couldn't wait to show it to the big cheeses. As I mentioned many pages ago, I began this presentation with such confidence that

I told the audience there was no use even bothering to talk to anyone else because my idea was untoppable. Two days later Liz got the "phone call." "We're going with someone else," the marketing staffer informed her, "we're going to go with a big-multiple-screen-multimedia-musical-montage-light-show-orgy." When she told me the news I became ill. I wasn't going to be able to produce my idea—my masterpiece. Eventually, Liz discovered our budget was six or seven times higher than what Sunbeam had allocated. Members of the marketing staff believed management would spend the bucks, but they were wrong. It was of little solace. I brooded for months.

Once you make your decision and hire a producer or writer, you enter the second phase of executive "producership"—you become the enabler. *Your mission is now to do whatever it takes to help the professionals you hired (directly and indirectly) do their best work.* It's your charge to encourage them, challenge them, push them . . . everything but do their job for them. I promise you, if you hired your producer or writer for all the right reasons, your chances of having a successful video are sky high.

6.5 MARKETING VIDEOS: UNDERSTANDING AND GUIDING THE CREATIVE AND PRODUCTION PROCESSES

I want to come to an understanding with you about the creative and production processes. I want you to understand that it takes imagination and experience to create a powerful marketing video; and while you may have a wonderful imagination, I assure you, you do not possess the experience needed to create even a mediocre video. By teaching you the rudiments of the creative and production processes, it's my hope that you will understand your role and responsibilities more clearly and gain greater respect for the professionals who practice this demanding craft.

Some of my peers argue that the video creative and production processes are separate and distinct disciplines; others believe they are a singular force. I am in the latter camp—admittedly because of my own predisposition to writing and directing. Consequently, we will look at the video creative/production process as one entity divided into four phases:

- ◆ Concept and script development.
- ◆ Preproduction.
- ◆ Production.
- ◆ Postproduction.

We will also take a more critical look at the executive producer's role in this process—a role that's especially pivotal at the video's inception.

Concept and Script Development

Concept and script development normally follow this course:

- Treatment.
- First draft (visual/audio).
- Revisions to first draft.
- Final script (prereview and approval by legal or other regulatory staff if necessary).
- Revisions to final script (if necessary).
- Production script.

Treatment

The treatment is an expanded concept statement. It defines the video—it overviews content and scene order and establishes the mood, style, pace, and tone of the finished video. There is no "standard" video treatment format; most producers adjust their treatments to the project at hand. (I looked over many of my old treatments while preparing this book and surprised myself at how dissimilar they were.) Treatments are generally developed by the producer, or by a writer, in concert with the producer.

As Executive Producer, the video treatment is where your input and scrutiny are most needed. *Take this responsibility seriously*—you can imagine the havoc you can create (not to mention the tab you can run up) by waiting until the production script has been written to finally pay attention to video's content, tone, style, and point of view. When reviewing a treatment you need to consider the following:

- Does the story line make sense or is it too contrived or too simplistic (will viewers tune out)?
- Is the story line interesting and informative (viewers' point of view)?
- Have all the key issues been addressed (content)?
- Have key points been properly emphasized?
- Is the tone and style consistent with the image of your organization?

Essentially, we are talking about the laws of clarity, comprehension, and impact with an audiovisual twist. Concern yourself with accuracy and net impression, don't try to be the creative director. Remember, you hired the producer for the *right* reasons—let the producer do the job he or she was hired to do.

Just as there is no standard treatment format, there is also no limit to the number of treatments (concepts) than can be created. To help illustrate that point, let's look a two treatments that were presented to Acme Foodservice Equipment's director of marketing. Acme is planning to launch a new mixer line, and a video has been proposed by both marketing and sales to support its introduction. (Please note: I am not trying to illuminate the differences between good and bad treatment writing—the fact is I've seen some very pedestrian treatments turned into spectacular videos. Unfortunately, I've seen an equal number exciting treatments turn out to be very pedestrian.)

Situation

Acme has planned a video to help support the introduction of its new variable-speed foodservice mixer line (VS-100 and VS-200). These types of mixers are used by bakeries and restaurants of all sizes and types (the restaurant market being much larger). The perennial leader, Hobart, is well entrenched (70 percent–plus share of market). However, Acme's new mixers have several features that make them superior to comparable Hobart models. Marketing really wants the video to make a fuss over these advantages—and the team wants to go toe-to-toe against Hobart. Additionally, marketing wants to place special emphasis on the top-of-the-line model VS-200. The following are product features/benefits:

1. Indirect drive/greater reliability, longer life.

2. Can't start out of gear/safety, less waste.

3. Power brake (standard)/safety.

4. Variable speed transmission/better mixing control, more options.

5. High-speed hub (50 percent faster)/greater productivity, longer shelf life, better looking presentation (less tearing, cleaner cut).

6. Welded heavy-gauge steel frame/durability.

7. Epoxy enamel finish/ease of cleaning.

8. Stainless steel bowls/longer-lasting, noncorrosive.

T R E A T M E N T 1

ACME VARIABLE SPEED MIXER
Unhappy Operator

INTRODUCTION

The video will tell a very comprehensive story of Acme's new mixer. Most of the action will take place in distributor/dealer's showroom, with other action occurring at Acme's research and development facility and in the prep area of a generic restaurant. Graphics and photography (primarily food shots) will support copy claims. A narrator will take us from scene to scene and help position Acme's mixer against Hobart's machine.

SCENE OVERVIEW

1. Open with shot of "owner" discussing his unhappiness over present mixer (Hobart) with his "baker." The owner claims he's "got to do something about it!"

2. Owner enters distributor showroom, explains situation to salesperson, and discusses *why* he is unhappy with current mixer.

3. Salesperson conducts feature/benefit comparison between Hobart and Acme (VS-200) mixer. (Camera will support salesperson's narrative with extreme close-up views.)

4. Salesperson will also use Acme sales literature and point-of-sale material in order to strengthen feature/benefit comparison. This material will come "alive" through limited animation techniques and "visits" to Acme's engineering lab. Cuts to beautiful color food photography will also support dialogue.

5. Video concludes with owner happily using his new Acme variable speed mixer (VS-200).

TONE

Video will be fast paced and feature lots of quick cuts and bright graphics. A music track will add memorability to story as well as facilitate scene and mood changes.

TREATMENT 2

ACME VARIABLE SPEED MIXER
Bob and Mary

INTRODUCTION

The video will employ two principal on-camera characters: an operator (Bob) of a "traditional" but contemporary full-service type restaurant (Bob and Mary's) and a dealer salesperson (Mike). Effectively this
is a problem/solution video. Mary's off-camera *voice only* will be used as
a device to help set up scenes as well as add a touch of light, good-
natured humor to increase viewer interest and awareness. The video
sells *directly* against Hobart; it highlights the features of indirect-drive
and variable-speed operations, stressing the key benefits of Acme's
new mixer: product quality/reliability, food quality/presentation,
greater safety, increased productivity, and efficiency.

GENERAL STORY LINE

1. We establish scene and situation: (a) restaurant exterior and
   interior; (b) the existence of (good natured) tension in Bob and
   Mary's relationship and; (c) that Bob is happy with his Acme
   VS-200 mixer.

2. Bob reflects back to a time when "things weren't quite so rosy,"
   to establish problem. Bob and Mary's mixer problem will be
   satirically highlighted with a "safe disaster" (e.g., their Hobart
   mixer explodes without harming anyone).

3. We again go back in time, on this occasion to learn how Bob and
   Mary solved their problem. Here we meet Mike, their Acme
   dealer salesperson. Ensuing action occurs back of house as Mike
   takes Bob (and Mary, off-camera) through the product, talking
   about and illustrating product features and benefits while
   making direct comparisons to Hobart. Use of props by Mike
   (e.g., indirect-drive gear) and cutaways to live and limited
   computer-generated animation graphics will be employed to
   make the features-and-benefits demonstrations more
   memorable.

4. Final scene returns to present. Bob succinctly reinforces key
   benefits of mixer. His final interplay with Mary teases viewers
   into believing they will *finally* get to see her. They won't.

Now, using the evaluation criteria I've just discussed with you, let's be Acme Foodservice Equipment's director of marketing and assess these two treatments. (I should point out that treatments often have a background or situation section up front, which I did not include in the two sample treatments you just reviewed.)

Story Line *Does the story line make sense or is it too contrived or too simplistic?* Because this is such a subjective question you need to ask yourself the following questions:

1. Are you in touch with the pop culture of your audience?
2. Would business people you respect refer to you as creative or imaginative with respect to marketing communications concepts?
3. Do you honestly like the work of the writer or producer you are working with?

If you answered no to either questions 1 or 2, and yes to question 3, you should give the benefit of the doubt to the writer or producer unless you're fairly certain the audience might be offended or misled. Reflect confidence in the skills of the professionals you've chosen to work with (at least until proven otherwise; ultimately, the audience will tell you if the video is a success or a bust). I would suggest that a *good* professional writer and/or director should be able to turn both of these story lines into solid videos. Now, note your comments and see if you and I are in agreement.

Unhappy Operator
Overall, I don't think the writer gave us a very good mental picture of the video. The overview of the story line was too general for my liking. I wouldn't sign off on this treatment until I had more information—I'd need to know more about the restaurant owner: his age, color, sex; his character—is he Mr. Serious, Joe Average, witty, friendly? I'd also like more information about the narrator: gender, tone of voice, specific role. I'm also not happy with the fact that I don't know if the "owner" runs a bakery or a restaurant. I don't think viewers will be able to relate as well to a generic owner as they will to a baker or restaurant operator—I'd rather commit to one or the other. (If justifiable, I would consider creating a version for bakeries and a version for restaurants.) Bottom line: Although the story line is somewhat predictable, I'd be comfortable in producing it as long as I had more character and scene detail—and a top-flight director.

Bob and Mary

Humor is always dangerous. Here the writer is using satire, and a little shtick, to reach viewers in an unconventional (memorable) fashion. Given the fact that Acme is going up against the undisputed market leader, satire could be an inspired approach. I'd want to be sure the writer and director have experience producing "humorous" marketing videos that were considered intelligent (clever or witty) not sophomoric. Finally, casting is *always* important, but it never gets more important than when you're casting for roles that require comic acting. For a marketing video of this type to be successful the actors must be engaging, believable, and likable (remember, everyone loved the Bunkers—even Archie). I'd be most interested in the talent my producer recommends; I'd want to see the audition tape or view sample reels.

Interest Level   *Is the story line interesting and informative?* The question is also subjective, even though it needs to be answered from the *audience's point of view* (a subject we've discussed at length). Keep in mind, you want the video to grab the audience and then hold their attention. Both video treatments essentially take the same "operator problem/solution" track. Videos that allow viewers to *identify* with fictional heroes, and the problems and tribulations they endure, usually hold viewer interest.

Unhappy Operator

This video is about as straightforward as you can get. Clearly, viewers will identify with the problems of the unhappy operator (if they don't, somebody better make sure there really is a market for this product). The video also will provide a platform for making viewers more knowledgeable about mixers in general and the difference between Acme and Hobart mixers in particular. There is a danger of getting too bogged down in details (which are usually more meaningful if left to the presenter to review with the customer or prospect). You'll be able to make that determination after you see a first draft of the video script.

Bob and Mary

With respect to problem solving, I could make the same comments about this treatment as I did for Unhappy Operator. On the other hand, I think the device of exaggeration and humor (if done well) will both *encourage* and *maintain* a high level of viewer interest. I also believe the video has the potential to create a favorable net impression of Acme (nontraditional, innovative, creative, etc.).

Key Issues   *Have all the key issues been addressed?* Nothing tricky about this question. Your job here is to make sure there are no glaring omissions in the treatment. Do the two treatments we just reviewed pass this test?

Unhappy Operator

The fact is this is pretty much a one issue video: a features-and-benefits comparison of "us versus them." This video certainly addresses that issue, but does it take on Hobart with sufficient impact? I'd push my writer on that point.

Bob and Mary

Does the VS-200 get enough attention or does it get lost in the device? Be sure that you're comfortable with the answer to that question.

Key Points *Have key points been properly emphasized?* The key word here is *emphasized.* You want to be sure the video covers the high points and stimulates viewer interest to learn more about the product or service being sold (specific information and questions that only a knowledgeable presenter can respond to). How do those treatments fare?

Unhappy Operator

Related to my concern about too many feature/benefits is a companion concern about the *impact* of the features and benefits the video will present. To that point, I'm intrigued by the idea of beautiful food photography. I believe restaurant operators and bakers will react positively to those images—I especially want viewers to relate "beautiful food" to Acme mixers. The treatment does not say *how* food photography will be used in the video—a subject I'd want to discuss in greater detail with the writer or producer before moving to a first draft.

Bob and Mary

I think the setup of the problem and how Acme's mixer "solves" the problem is interesting and fun. But the treatment does not do a good enough job of explaining how key features and benefits will be stressed. Moreover, I know the inherent danger of using humor—the risk that the "jokes" will fall flat, be offensive, or get in the way of the product story. An experienced writer and director will make me feel a lot less nervous about that risk.

Tone and Style *Is the tone and style consistent with the image of your organization?* This question is not as subjective as it appears. Your company's persona rests somewhere on the image continuum between investment-banker-conservative-gray (the right) and silicon-valley-free-wheeling-tie-dyed (the left). You generally do not want to stray too far from your established image (unless your company has made a strategic decision to do so). However, "conservative" companies don't need to create dry, boring marketing communications, and everything a free-wheeling organization produces doesn't have to be off-the-wall. But there is one maxim I suggest you do follow: Bad taste is always in bad taste. Are either of our treatments in bad taste?

Unhappy Operator

As pointed out earlier, this approach is pretty conservative (traditional). Good production values, good writing, good graphics, great food photography, and good acting will make it a very good video. If you want to push the video one way or the other (to the left or right), inform your producer or writer of your desire. He or she will adjust characters, sets, scenes, and copy accordingly.

Bob and Mary

I'm a little concerned about the sexist stereotyping of the video ("nagging wife"), but I could be convinced that the satirical nature of the video will dispel that worry. (Does anyone take Curly, Larry, or Moe seriously?) On the other hand, if my company is pretty conservative, I might ask the writer to consider other options. I'm also not so sure we want a Hobart to blow up. (I'd bet the legal department would have a collective coronary.) Consequently, I'd caution the writer to be sure the "safe disaster" is not libelous.

Sorry, but it doesn't matter to me if you agree or disagree with my impressions of these treatments. What *does* matter to me is that you recognize *how critical it is for you to carefully consider and evaluate a video treatment against a fixed criteria.* I want you to be rewarded by your video, not victimized by it—and the best way to do that is to be sure your creative team is pointed in the right direction.

Before we leave the subject of treatments, I want to talk about one of the most common marketing video formats, "talking heads." A *talking-head* video is best described (at the extreme) as a speech or lecture captured on videotape. Better talking-head videos incorporate cutaways to graphics (charts, maps, copy points) or "B roll" to enhance the speaker's presentation by adding interest, energy, and memorability. (*B roll* refers to visuals that support dialogue or establish locations, moods, etc.; for example, if a customer talks about how easy a product is to service, the producer may want to edit in a shot that illustrates that claim.) I introduced the subject of talking-heads because more than enough *bad* videos of this type have already been produced—I don't want you to add to the pile. If you're planning to produce a talking-head video be sure your treatment calls for lots of interesting and energetic cutaways.

First Draft

Following approval of the treatment, you will be given a first draft of the script to review and critique. The video script contains both audio and visual information. The audio information consists of all on- and off-camera dialogue, music (intros, outros, stings, and beds), and sound effects. Video information includes descriptions of camera shots, ranging from general ("in an office") to very specific ("standing next to an operating punch press while the press operator loads in a new steel coil . . ."), as well as the nature of the shot (close-up, long shot, montage, etc.). Video information also includes all animation sequences, charts and graphs, and titling. First drafts are occasionally accompanied by storyboards (usually "rough pencils"), outlining some, or even all, of the key scenes. For example, if your video includes a computer-generated animation sequence, the producer will want to be sure the animation story is both accurate and compelling. You can expect to see pencils and several key frames in sufficient detail for comment and approval. (Hint: Think of animation sequences as productions within the production.)

The first draft of the video script is the offspring of the treatment. And like any newborn, it requires special attention. But before you can intelligently comment on a video script, you have to know how to read one. Let's look at a portion of a first draft of "Bob and Mary."

Client: Acme International/Foodservice Equipment Division
Project: Acme VS Mixer Market Intro Video
Date: May 21, 1997
Draft: 1

1. FU TO DAYTIME EXTERIOR OF "URBAN/ TRENDY" RESTAURANT (BOB AND MARY'S). XF TO 2 OR 3 RESTAURANT INTERIORS.	(Ambient Sounds and Bright Music Under)
2. CUT TO LS BACK OF HOUSE. BOB IS ENGAGED IN HIS WORK WHILE STANDING NEXT TO "PURRING" ACME VS-200 MIXER. SCENE ESTABLISHES. CAMERA MOVES TO MCU BOB.	(Music Fades Out) MARY (OS): (Shrilly) Bob!!!!!!! We need more jalapeño biscuits, we're running out!
3. BOB REACTS, TURNS TO CAMERA, SMILES AND PATS VS-200.	BOB (OC): Yep, things are running pretty smoothly now—but it wasn't so long ago . . . (Bob Reflects).

4. RIPPLE DISS TO SAME (BUT "DINGIER") KITCHEN WITH BOB LOOKING HARASSED AND FRUSTRATED. WE SEE HIM HASTILY ADD MASHED POTATO INGREDIENTS TO HOBART MIXER.	MARY (OS):(Shrilly) Bob!!!!!!!! We're running out of the cilantro-horseradish-asiago mashed potatoes—you'd better move it!!!!
5. SERIES OF QUICK RELATED-ACTION CUTS OF BOB SETTING OUT TO "FIRE UP" THE MIXER CLIMAXING IN "DISASTER" —THE MIXER'S CONTENTS SPEW OUT OF BOWL AND LAND ALL OVER KITCHEN . . . AND BOB.	MARY (OS):(Unintelligible Shrieking)
6. RESOLVE TO ECU OF "STEAMED," PARTIALLY WHIPPED-POTATO-FACED BOB	
7. MATCH RIPPLE DISS BACK TO PRESENT; day; BOB SMILES TO HIMSELF RECALLING INCIDENT. BOB TURNS TO CAMERA AND NODS KNOWINGLY.	BOB (OC): Yeah, I remember that that was the day I called Mike and told him I wanted to shoot my Hobart (heh, heh) and . . . (We Hear Mary Shriek), and uh, that he'd better get down here right away!
8. ECU BOB	BOB (OC): (Joyfully) That's when I first learned about the *Acme Alternative;* it was one of the happiest days of my life.
9. RIPPLE DISS TO SAME KITCHEN DAY OF DELIVERY OF VS-200 (MIKE IS PRESENT WITH BOB); BOB APPEARS TO BE RETELL- ING HIS "POTATO FACE" ADVENTURE.	MIKE (OC): You know Bob, this mixer could never start out of gear it has . . .

The above script is a common script format: visual information on the left, audio information on the right. (The following illustrates a portion of that same script in "stacked" format.)

Client: Acme International/Foodservice Equipment Division
Project: Acme VS Mixer Market Intro Video
Date: May 21, 1997
Draft: 1

1. FU TO DAYTIME EXTERIOR OF "URBAN/TRENDY" RESTAURANT (BOB AND MARY'S). XF TO 2 OR 3 RESTAURANT INTERIORS.
   (Ambient Sounds and Bright Music Under)

2. CUT TO LS BACK OF HOUSE. BOB IS ENGAGED IN HIS WORK WHILE STANDING NEXT TO "PURRING" ACME VS-200 MIXER. SCENE ESTABLISHES. CAMERA MOVES TO MCU BOB.
   (Music Fades Out)

MARY (OS): (Shrilly) Bob!!!!!!! We need more jalapeño biscuits, we're running out!

3. BOB REACTS, TURNS TO CAMERA, SMILES AND PATS VS-200.

BOB (OC): Yep, things are running pretty smoothly now—but it wasn't so long ago . . . (Bob Reflects).

4. RIPPLE DISS TO SAME (BUT "DINGIER") KITCHEN WITH BOB LOOKING HARASSED AND FRUSTRATED. WE SEE HIM HASTILY ADD MASHED POTATO INGREDIENTS TO HOBART MIXER.

MARY (OS):(Shrilly) Bob!!!!!!!! We're running out of the cilantro-horseradish-asiago mashed potatoes—you'd better move it!!!!

5. SERIES OF QUICK RELATED-ACTION CUTS OF BOB SETTING OUT TO "FIRE UP" THE MIXER CLIMAXING IN "DISASTER"—THE MIXER'S CONTENTS SPEWS OUT OF BOWL AND LAND ALL OVER KITCHEN . . . AND BOB.

MARY (OS): (Unintelligible Shrieking)

6. RESOLVE TO ECU OF "STEAMED," PARTIALLY WHIPPED-POTATO-FACED BOB.

7. MATCH RIPPLE DISS BACK TO PRESENT; BOB SMILES TO HIMSELF RECALLING INCIDENT. BOB TURNS TO CAMERA AND NODS.

BOB (OC): Yeah, I remember that day, that was the day I called Mike and told him I wanted to shoot my Hobart (heh, heh) and . . . (We Hear Mary Shriek), and uh, that he'd better get down here right away!

8. ECU BOB

BOB (OC): (Joyfully) That's when I first learned about the *Acme Alternative;* it was one of the happiest days of my life.

9. RIPPLE DISS TO SAME KITCHEN DAY OF DELIVERY OF VS-200 (MIKE IS PRESENT WITH BOB); BOB APPEARS TO BE RETELLING HIS "POTATO FACE" ADVENTURE.

MIKE (OC): You know Bob, this mixer could never start out of gear it has . . .

However, format isn't the issue—being able to properly read the script *is*. First of all many readers may not be familiar with script information shorthand. Here's a list of the most common abbreviations:

FO	fade out
FU	fade up
XF	cross fade
DISS	dissolve
ZO	zoom out
ZI	zoom in
IO	iris out
II	iris in
PL	pan left

PR	pan right
TU	tilt up
TD	tilt down
D	dolly (means of rigging camera on "tracks" to follow action)
WS	wide shot
LS	long shot
MLS	medium-long shot
MS	medium shot
MCU	medium close-up
CU	close-up
ECU	extreme close-up
VECU	very extreme close-up (also called a "choker")
2-S	two shot (direction to include two people in shot)
3-S	three shot (direction to include three people in shot)
OC	on-camera
OS	off-stage
VO	voice-over
ANNR	announcer
SFX	sound effect
MOT	silent (without sound)

Reviewing a first-draft video script is painless. Usually the producer and/or writer will be present to overview (introduce) the script and answer your questions. I suggest you follow this procedure for reviewing first drafts:

1. Read the script in its entirety (make a brief note of anything that's unclear).

2. Get clarification on visual or audio information you didn't understand.

3. Consider the treatment. The most important question to ask yourself is, Did the writer successfully breathe life into the treatment? If not, you need to determine what is amiss—and why.

4. Review and consider each of the scenes (video and audio) carefully. Do they make "sense" individually, and do they mesh together to tell a cohesive story?

Reading the Left Side of the Script (video)   I find it helpful to read the video information without reading the audio; this method gives me a better sense of visual continuity. Think in terms of communications objectives; don't get "hung up" with camera direction or effects. (These directions are usually perfunctory in first drafts anyhow; experienced writers are more concerned with story continuity and visualization of key points.) Focus on the *completeness, impact, practicality, accuracy,* and *integrity* of the proposed visuals. Be sure all the information you want imparted to viewers is present and accounted for. If you can suggest more dramatic or memorable ways to make a point, express those ideas. If visuals are misleading or inaccurate, correct them. If the writer is calling for action that is impossible (or too costly) to execute, advise and suggest alternatives. Finally, check over charts and graphs for accuracy, legibility, etc. (You know what to look for in good charts and graphs, right?)

Reading the Right Side of the Script (audio)   I also like to read the audio portion of the script by itself—this helps give me a better feel for tone and flow—I suggest you do the same. You especially want to read and "listen to" the audio from the audience's point of view: Is the copy interesting, informative, compelling? Is the dialogue clear and realistic? Is the vocabulary appropriate?

   You may need to review certain portions of the script with experts (e.g., technical, legal, or medical staff). Be sure to do so in a timely manner; you don't want to delay production, or worse, move ahead only to later discover you need to reshoot. You also need to be concerned that details for taping of operations, products, or customers are addressed.

   Finally, please don't be one of those clods who runs around soliciting opinions on creative efforts from waiters, car parkers, bartenders, spouses, et al. by asking them what they think of the script. If you're unsure of your ability to judge the script and want a "second opinion" talk with someone you respect—someone who has experience with videos and a reasonable understanding of your business. But frankly, after you've read this book, you won't need help. People will be coming to you for advice.

Subsequent Script Revisions

Following review of the first draft, revisions will be made and submitted to you for approval—one or two more drafts are usually required. The final *approved* script becomes the production script. (Sometimes a "final" script needs to be cleared for production by company legal or regulatory departments.) The production script is what the producer and director will use as a blueprint to guide the construction of the video.

Preproduction

Bringing the production script to life is the principal task, and ideally, the joie de vivre, of the producer and director. But don't minimize *your* role in the video's preproduction phase.

Most of the technical decisions will not (and should not) require your involvement. But *do* be prepared to approve talent selection, locations, set designs, props, costumes, music, graphic styling, and what's for lunch because no producer or director ever wants to hear a client-cum-executive producer utter those dreaded words, "Hey! Wait a minute! What's that!? Who approved that!?"

All video budgets are based on assumptions made by the producer with respect to equipment, staging, time, and people resources. Now, the producer, director, and various experts (e.g., specialists in videography, lighting, music, etc.) need to address technical issues and agree on the specific utilization of those resources including: selecting videotaping locations, arranging talent auditions, producing music, designing sets, and securing permits.

Most producers I know boil preproduction down to problem solving and scheduling. The following elements are the most common and important preproduction issues that often require a good dose of problem solving.

Location *Location* refers to the site or sites where videotaping of scenes will occur. Good locations can add a great deal of interest and credibility to a video; conversely, uninspired, contrived locations impair the video's effectiveness. Videotaping usually takes place at a production studio (sound stage) or at an actual site (whence the phrase *on location*). Field locations are problematic: producers need to give attention to power supply, noise levels, availability, accessibility, and camera maneuverability. Sometimes even finding an acceptable location can be a hair-pulling experience (good location scouts are coveted). Frequently locations are givens, for example, one of your manufacturing or processing facilities or a customer's place of business. In those cases, it's preferable for the producer or director to visit the location before taping. (Be sure all appropriate managers are notified of the taping and scouting dates promptly to ensure maximum cooperation.) If unscripted interviews are being taped, it's almost mandatory to have the director visit the site prior to shooting. A "preinterview" with the person or people being taped will help the director conduct a better interview when the camera is rolling. It's been my experience that interviewees are usually more relaxed after having met and talked with the person who is going to interview them. It's not uncommon for you (the executive producer) or some member of the sponsoring company to be present at these interviews to ensure the answers to the questions are appropriate and that nothing has been overlooked.

Talent   People who are seen or heard on-camera, or whose voices are heard on the video, are collectively referred to as "talent." Talent can make or break a video. Talent can be divided into three general groups:

- *On-camera principals.* Professional actors or real people (e.g., employees or customers) who play a major role in the video.
- *Narrators or spokespersons.* Professional actors or real people who do not appear in front of the camera but help tell the story (also called "voice-over talent").
- *On-camera extras.* Professional actors or real people who may or may not deliver dialogue and play only minor roles in the video.

Your direction and involvement in the talent selection process is more significant than you might think. For example, if actors are to serve as spokespersons for your company, or to portray employees or customers, you will need to help establish character guidelines (age, color, sex, personality) for these people. Most producers will involve the director in the talent-selection process (principally because the director is the person responsible for the talent's performance). It usually isn't necessary for you to attend the casting session, but at the least, you will receive tapes or composites of selected talent for your approval. Your *primary* talent concern is with nonprofessionals, usually your own company employees or customers who have agreed to endorse your product or service. You want to be sure that they make a good impression and that what they say is consistent with the communications objectives of the video. I always suggest overtaping: If we think we need two or three employees to tell our story, I'll tape four or five (when possible); similarly, when taping "endorsers," I always like to get at least one more than we think we'll need. On several occasions we were thankful we had an extra testifier; you never know when someone will freeze up or become inarticulate in front of a camera.)

Set Design   The visual impression of the video is influenced by the character of the picture (video camera, lenses, filters, focal lengths, the "eye" of the videographer), the lighting, and the set itself. We need to consider set design from two perspectives: field locations and sound stages.

   ♦ *Field locations.* Usually, your reason for taping on location is to lend realism and credibility to the video. If taping is being done at your facilities, be sure the visuals make a positive impression on the audience. If you're taping on the premises of a customer or vendor, be sure to be sensitive to the company's needs and restrictions (such as, what and where you can shoot, who you can and cannot shoot, and how much time it is willing to allocate to you to complete the taping session). Frequently, field locations are transformed to look like something they're not: a test kitchen becomes a pizzeria; a lunchroom becomes a service center; an old dingy bar is transformed into a smoky pool room. You need to scrutinize those sets for accuracy of detail and appearance—phony looking sets are distracting and discrediting.

   ♦ *Sound stages.* Sound stages are like magic carpets. They can take you anyplace you care to be, as imaginatively or prosaically as you wish: to the surface of the moon, inside a human heart . . . in a customer's office, somewhere in limbo. At their most basic, sound stages are the backdrops of all those talking-head videos I referred to earlier; at their plushest, they can rival a Broadway musical or big budget movie.

   As always, your primary task is to help the professionals do their job. Use common sense; if a set looks inappropriate or unprofessional, express your concerns to the producer. Try to be specific, and remember, your job is to give impression and direction, not to come up with solutions.

Wardrobe and Makeup   As in casting talent, your role is to help establish guidelines relative to the general look of the talent. You want your employees, for example, to look natural and confident, not "staged." Producers always have talent bring several outfits (within a style) to give the director some latitude in case lighting or blending (of colors within a set) becomes an issue. Most production crews will have a makeup/hair stylist on set to obviate such nuisances as facial "hot spots," fly-away hair, or weird skin tones *and* to enhance the appearance of the on-camera talent. (You wouldn't want an important customer to look like the star of a "Don't Do Drugs" public service announcement or have big glare bouncing off his or her receding hairline.) A good makeup/hair stylist distinguishes a professionally produced video and strengthens its net impression.

Crew and Equipment   As promised, I will not discuss the advantages of Beta SP over SVHS or when to use a D-2 filter instead of a D-3 or which wireless microphones work best in cold weather. As far as crews are concerned, don't be mislead by all those credits that roll (it seems forever) at the end of a motion picture. Video crews are generally small in number, the most basic being an electronic news-gathering (ENG) crew. An ENG crew typically consists of a videographer (camera operator), gaffer (lighting), and video engineer (audio and picture). Beyond a videographer, gaffer, and engineer, a video production may require grips (people to move or rig equipment, lights, sets, or props), a makeup/hair stylist, a teleprompter operator, or one or two other specialists. Fundamentally, you have to trust the judgment of your producer when it comes to crew and equipment. But there is one aspect of crew and equipment I do want you to be alert to: competitive bidding (should you choose that option). Before you hire the lowest bidder be sure to scrutinize the bid carefully, especially the equipment and crew specifications. If major differences exist among the bidders, this area is usually where you'll find them. You should feel free to ask the low bidder why specific items weren't included. If you're not fully comfortable with the answers (especially if you get a couple of "we must have overlooked that" or "we don't *think* we'll need it"), you may be getting "low balled" or the producer was just plain careless. Either way, you may want to think about hiring the next-to-lowest bidder.

Animation   In my experience, animation is the single biggest cause of going over budget. You can avoid such unpleasantness by giving your producer clear and complete direction, as well as spending the time to review storyboards carefully. I always like to have one or two short animation segments produced so that my clients (and I) have the opportunity to view and evaluate the finished animation before moving forward with the entire production. I assure you, this step can save time and money.

Music   Music is rarely over budget. I'm already on record as being an advocate of original music (which is not nearly as expensive as many people believe)—I hope to make you a fellow advocate. Producers who balk over the use of stock music are cognizant of the fact that music is often the difference between a good video and a *memorable* video. Be a good enabler, help create memorable videos (and whistle a happy tune).

If I failed to make it clear, preproduction meetings encompass every aspect of the video production. The preproduction meeting also generates the production schedule—a document the producer holds sacred. I have repeatedly stated that powerful videos are not made overnight. Be sensitive to the fact that even the best planned productions, managed by experienced professionals, can run into unforeseen calamities. Consequently, you should make every effort to build extra time into the production schedule. (Smart producers *always* build extra time in their schedules.) You'll be glad you did.

Production

Lights! Camera! Action! At last, the glamour and glitz you've been waiting for.

Sorry. As some of you may already know, all that glamour and glitz is just another Hollywood myth. The truth is that video production is usually boring for just about everyone but the director, crew, and talent (and even they can grow restless at times). Frankly, it's not uncommon to spend *hours* taping 20 or 30 *seconds* of action. Sets take time to prepare and properly light. Talent needs to be rehearsed and then taped or filmed until the director is comfortable with the performances and camera work. More hours may pass as sets are torn down and new ones set up. And then there are the production gremlins—unknown forces that cause equipment failures and other misadventures. Meanwhile, in trendy lofts in some arty part of town animation artists are rendering your examples, comparisons, charts, and graphs; musicians are working on the score of a dramatic opening; model makers are creating miniatures of your newest product features. Everything you helped inspire and initiate is now in process, moving inexorably to completion.

The production process is largely the domain of the producer. The producer will be worrying about logistics, scheduling, budgets, and the overall quality and effectiveness of the visual and audio elements being created. But you're not necessarily "off duty." Your active involvement (or the involvement of company experts whom you may designate) may still be required during the production phase, especially at recording sessions (voice-over or on-camera) where correct pronunciation and proper emphasis are essential or at the videotaping of customer testimonials (to ensure that all the questions have been asked and answered satisfactorily). You will be asked to check and approve a myriad of details; most of these approvals will be perfunctory, but occasionally you'll be asked to make some tough choices. In those cases, your producer will usually be able to explain the options, describe the consequences of your decision, and offer advice. But the final say belongs to you. Try your best to make those calls with the idea of making the video work harder for you—with the idea of making a more powerful video. To that point, allow me to offer another of my power presentation maxims: Everyone will *eventually* forget if you went over budget if the video is well done and even moderately successful. But *no one* will ever forget if you create an abomination or embarrassment that fails miserably in the marketplace. Trust me on this one.

Postproduction
Editing is the final and decisive step to creating a powerful video.

When all the video and audio elements have been produced, you are (literally) in the hands of the editor to bring the video to life. Editing a video in the digital age is somewhat different in practice, but not in principle, from the days when 16mm film was the gold standard of business visual communications (industrial films). The postproduction process generally follows this course: First the video, in whole or part, is rough cut (a no-frills edit that I'll cover in more depth momentarily) for the executive producer's review and approval. A second, or even third, rough cut may be needed to reflect revisions or add elements (e.g., music or graphics) that were not included in the original rough cut. Once the rough cut has been approved, the final edit is then executed.

At the postproduction stage, you can really do very little, short of having scenes reshot, voice-over talent or music rerecorded, or animation and graphics rerendered, to materially affect the video. (These changes are also known as very expensive second guessing).

Nevertheless, having a general understanding of what's going on in the postproduction phase is desirable if you want to become an "reward winning" executive producer. The following brief overview of the postproduction process will help you attain that objective.

Rough Cut   Rarely, if ever, is a video shot beginning to end (chronologically) as written in the production script; for example, all scenes that take place in a particular location, or on a specific set, are shot at the same time as a matter of efficiency. Consequently, the producer's first job is to be sure the *core* video and audio elements tell a coherent story, which is accomplished by producing a full or partial rough cut of the video. The producer begins by reviewing all the footage that was shot, selects the best takes, and cuts them together (usually) without including visual effects, music, graphics, titles, and B roll in order to be certain the video flows smoothly. The rough cut is then presented to the executive producer for review and comment. You should concentrate *only* on the content of the video, not the aesthetics (that comes later). Is it logical? Does it tell your story effectively and powerfully?

The process varies somewhat for videos that include nonscripted interviews (testimonials in particular). In those cases the producer selects the best takes from the interviews and reviews them with the executive producer in order to prioritize the comments of the person or people interviewed (ranging from "must be in the video" to "include if possible" to "don't even think about it"). Those takes are then rough cut into the "story" that was outlined in the production script. Sometimes narrator copy is written and recorded *after* the interviews have been cut together to help underscore key points and/or segue between scenes. Music, graphics, and titles may also be created after the rough cut has been reviewed and approved.

Final Edit   Walking into a modern-day video-edit suite is like walking into the space shuttle—you are immediately overwhelmed by decks, switches, panels, monitors, lights, and gadgets of every sort. Edit sessions can often be just as tedious as sound-stage or location production. And yes, there are editing gremlins, who can be just as insidious as their cousins, the production gremlins. In spite of all that, I encourage you to attend a final (on-line) edit session, at least once, in order to gain a "feel" for the process. (Once is usually more than enough.) Watching a skilled editor assemble the video elements into a smooth, seamless story is truly an experience.

You and your producer will evaluate the finished edit qualitatively: the visual images, graphics, audio clarity, music, and richness of color. Now is the time to fine-tune the video and resolve those issues. Once approved, the final edited version serves as a production master from which all subsequent copies will be made. Your next task will be to introduce the video to your sales and marketing people, show them how to turn that video into a powerful selling tool, and motivate them to use it. With a great video, that job is easy.

You are now sufficiently informed, and I hope eager, to create a powerful marketing video. Refer to this chapter throughout the process, and I'm confident you'll produce a video you'll be proud to show to any customer or prospect. Write to me and let me know how the video performed—who knows, my next book may be on video-marketing success stories.

7

Working with Creative Resources

7.1 WORKING WITH CREATIVE RESOURCES: MAKING IT SWEET

Recognizing that a great deal of the success of powerful business presentations rests in the hands of creative resources ("creative types"), I thought it would be a good idea to give you some insight into these people. I know many corporate executive types who consider working with creative people one of the most satisfying and enjoyable aspects of their job. Knowing how to effectively manage and motivate creative types can be a very rewarding experience (both personally and professionally). Consider this brief chapter "an instruction manual" for the care and nurturing of creative resources. Please read carefully before assembling your presentation.

"I Wouldn't Have Thought of That in a Million Years!"

Creative types are commonly viewed by mainstream business folks as being a bit odd (except for the high-profile, filthy-rich ones who are regarded as eccentric). I entreat you not to casually dismiss or minimize the value of these resources by limiting them to merely executing *your* ideas. The people or organizations who make their livings as

177

commercial artists—the writers, graphic designers, art directors, photographers, musicians, film makers, and others of this ilk—can frequently contribute mightily to the cause.

The archetypal creative type was usually the best artist in sixth grade, a precocious class clown, or editor of the school paper. Many of these people are exceptionally bright and highly skilled. The very best among them look beyond traditional solutions and consistently challenge conventional wisdom. They are exactly the kind of people you want involved in your projects. The following is my preferred way of working with creative resources.

Getting the Most from Your Creative Resources—Part 1: Before the Fact

1. *Talk directly with the person or people who will be responsible for the conceptual thinking and execution at the onset of the project— accept no substitutes.*

I'm sorry if this advice irritates account executives or other intermediaries of creative resources, but it is truly the way I believe information and ideas should be presented. If you're working with an external marketing support organization (e.g., ad agency, PR firm, marketing communications group) or an in-house "agency," don't allow yourself to be insulated from the person or people who have creative responsibility for your project. Would you be surprised if I told you that more often than not the information imparted to the creative types by account executive types is miscommunicated? Of course you wouldn't. In fact, you can bet that at least 50 percent of what you tell account people will not be recounted at all. It's tough for creative people to do their best work with incomplete and edited information.

2. *Be enthusiastic. Get your creative resources to invest in your project.*

Enthusiasm is infectious. You want the creative people who will be working on your project to know that this project means a lot to you and that you're relying on them to help you make it successful. Let them feel your energy and emotions—let them know how badly you want it. Let them inhale all the nuances an account executive, no matter how good he or she may be, could never really capture. Get them involved.

3. *Tell them what you want to accomplish, not what to do.*

Before getting into the details of the project, you must clearly state your objectives and be sure your creative resources comprehend them. Knowing what you want to accomplish helps keep everyone—them and you—focused on the goals. Telling creative types what to do and how to do it is demotivating; in effect you're asking them to be order takers, not creative thinkers. Too bad, because you'll never see ideas or directions that could dwarf your own.

4. *Give them lots of fodder and get them to ask lots of questions.*

You can't give your creative resources too much quality information. Remember, you need to keep focusing on the objectives. Tell your creative resources all you can about the audience—what turns them on, what turns them off. Give them any (relevant/current) existing materials you have that deal with the subject at hand (e.g., promotional literature, technical data, fact sheets, research papers). It's important to spark their interests, stimulate their imaginations, and rouse their curiosities. Be sure they understand that you want them to ask questions. Asking questions gets them to start thinking about your project and concentrating their creative energies on solutions. (If you've done that, you got 'em just where you want 'em.)

5. *Share your ideas.*

Don't be timid about espousing any ideas you may have regarding creative concepts. By all means, present your ideas as fully (and as enthusiastically) as possible. On the other hand, don't be defensive or discouraged. You can expect criticism and flat out rejection.

6. *Challenge them.*

Tell your creative resources you don't want conventional, trite solutions. Challenge them to create something distinctive, intelligent, and hard-hitting. Dare them to blow you away.

Getting the Most from Your Creative Resources—Part 2: After the Fact

1. *Respect their ideas.*

It's one of the oldest rules in the book: "do unto others . . ." I think it's reasonable to assume you expect your business associates to give you the courtesy of listening to your ideas and thoughts—to allow you to elaborate, clarify, and respond to their questions. Surely your creative resources deserve the same consideration. Give it to them.

2. *Be objective.*

I have written a great deal about the art of evaluating creative output. I've urged you to keep an open mind, to measure ideas against objectives, and to always take the audience's point of view. I realize that remaining objective isn't easy. It's difficult to filter out your biases and ignore your predispositions; consequently, you need to evaluate your evaluations. Use this test. If your reasons for rejecting an idea or concept aren't supported by solid business reasons, you're not being objective. Unsupportable objections include "Yeah, but *this* audience is different." "I don't like blue." "My wife hated it." "My husband hated it." "My significant other hated it." "So, if it's such a good idea, how come no one else thought of it?" I hope these examples make you cringe. Good creative people will "shut down" when their work is rejected irrationally or fatuously; alternatively, they will respond in a positive manner when the reasons for the rejection are substantive. Recognizing when and if you've lost your objectivity is one of the secrets to mastering the art of evaluating creative output.

3. *Be Considerate.*

Ideas must stand the test of objective scrutiny. Some ideas or concepts are so obviously good they light up the room. High fives all around. But what about ideas that can be supportably criticized? First, be sure your conclusions are correct. Sometimes further explanations and refinements can make ideas, written off as moribund, positively sparkle. But when ideas are off the mark, you're faced with the unenviable task of redirecting and remotivating your creative resources. Begin by identifying exactly *what is unacceptable and why it's unacceptable* in as much detail as possible. I suggest not dwelling on negatives. Focus on the positives—you want to build from strength. Be encouraging. Suggest specific directions to pursue or areas to explore. Don't lose your enthusiasm (at least publicly). If you're really concerned, keep it to yourself but do seek the counsel of other creative resources (especially if you've lost confidence, waiting until the 11th hour to make a move could be disastrous).

Thank You

Most of the time, if your creative resources are qualified and properly motivated and directed, you're going to get back very good work. Don't forget to tell the people responsible for that very good work how pleased you are with their efforts. Everyone likes to be recognized for doing a good job. Creative types are especially keen on getting feedback (positive or negative). It's one of the reasons they do what they do.

Finally, don't lose sight of the fact that coming up with good ideas is only half the job. Turning those good ideas into powerful presentations is the ultimate goal. Fortunately, turning good ideas into powerful presentations is what this book is all about. Keep it handy.

INDEX